CAN YOU LET GO OF A GRUDGE?

Can You Let Go of a Grudge?

LEARN TO FORGIVE AND GET ON WITH YOUR LIFE

FRANK DESIDERIO, CSP

Paulist Press
New York / Mahwah, NJ

Extract from the poem "The Sleeping Man Is Blessed," appearing p. xiv, from the Penguin publication *Love Poems from God*, copyright 2002 by Daniel Ladinsky and used with his permission.

The Scripture quotations contained herein are from the New Revised Standard Version: Catholic Edition, Copyright © 1989 and 1993, by the Division of Christian Education of the National Council of the Churches of Christ in the United States of America. Used by permission. All rights reserved.

Cover image by Alex Emanuel Koch / Shutterstock.com
Cover and book design by Lynn Else

Library of Congress Cataloging-in-Publication Data

Desiderio, Frank R.
    Can you let go of a grudge? : learn to forgive and get on with your life / Frank Desiderio, CSP.
        pages cm
    ISBN 978-0-8091-4844-8 (alk. paper) — ISBN 978-1-58768-293-3
    1. Forgiveness—Religious aspects—Christianity. I. Title.
    BV4647.F55D48 2014
    234`.5—dc23

                                                                    2013043247

ISBN 978-0-8091-4844-8 (paperback)
ISBN 978-1-58768-293-3 (e-book)

Published by Paulist Press
997 Macarthur Boulevard
Mahwah, New Jersey 07430

www.paulistpress.com

Printed and bound in the
United States of America

CONTENTS

To my father and mother,
Frank and Mary Desiderio,
who provided me with the
first school of mercy and justice.

ACKNOWLEDGMENTS

Much of what I know about forgiveness, both theoretical and practical, I learned from working on the documentary *The Big Question: A Film About Forgiveness*. I learned the theory from the psychologists, theologians, scientists, and practitioners of forgiveness. I had to practice forgiveness as a response to the stressful and conflict-ridden process of making the movie. In the economy of God's irony, if you want to learn about forgiveness then make a movie about it.

I am indebted to Dr. Everett Worthington for his insights about forgiveness and down-to-earth applications of its practice. I'd like to acknowledge Gus Reininger, who helped get the project off the ground. I'd like to thank the staff of Paulist Productions, particularly Joseph Kim, Enid Sevilla, and Barbara Gangi, who gave invaluable help along the way. Especially, I must offer my gratitude to Ria Aldanese, who was my second brain and source of good cheer. I need to thank Kaluska Poventude, who took the project on as producer and cared for it like a mother. I want to thank the great documentarian Vince DiPersio, who shaped the film and launched it into the world. I am indebted to all the people who have participated in the forgiveness seminars and retreats that I've led since making the movie. They have inspired me by their grace-filled acts of forgiveness. This book grew out of the film and those retreats. Paulist Fathers Larry Boadt (1942–2010) and Mark-David Janus believed in the project and said yes to the book. Finally, my thanks to Donna Crilly, who provided invaluable editorial insights and patient corrections.

FORGIVENESS PRAYER

Lord Jesus, our brother,
you were betrayed by your friends
and know the deepest pain of human sin;
from the cross you said, "Father, forgive them."

You taught us to pray to our Father,
"forgive us our trespasses
as we forgive those who trespass against us."

You are the Lord of justice,
help us to tell the truth
and live it.
You are the compassion of God,
help us to show mercy
and mean it.
You are the divine healer,
help us to forgive
and feel it.

We pray this in the power of the Holy Spirit
who is our strength to let go of the past,
our courage to grow into our best selves. Amen.

Frank Desiderio, CSP

INTRODUCTION

Have you ever felt eaten up by resentment? Is your spirit held hostage to some hurt? Has someone insulted you and now you keep thinking about it and chewing on it like a dog with a tasty bone?

Perhaps you keep rolling around in your head hurtful comeback lines to speak when someone has wounded you. Or maybe you've suffered a deep betrayal when a loved one has lied to you or left you, and you can't get past the hurt and move on with your life.

Often in the midst of such a problem, a well-meaning friend says to you, "Just let it go." And you think, "I'd love to do that. Want to tell me how?"

That's what this book is about: how to "let go" when you are wrestling with resentment, when you hold a grudge and can't seem—or don't want—to let it loose. This book is about slipping out of the grip of your past so that you can look back with peace and move forward.

WHAT IS THE BIG QUESTION?

After people have seen the film *The Big Question: A Film About Forgiveness*, which I produced, they ask me, "What is The Big Question?" The question I was thinking of when we named the film is "Can you forgive?" Later, I thought, sometimes the better question is "Should you forgive, or not?" So there is more than one big question; which big question depends on the time of your life. For now, the first big question to ask yourself is "Will I let go of the past?" That is, do I want to let go so that I can move into a future brighter than the past? If there is no true willingness to let go, then you can never loosen your grip.

Can You Let Go of a Grudge? will help you examine forgiveness and better understand and put into practice a spirituality of forgiveness. The book will guide you through the issues that get in the way of forgiving someone and show you a five-step process to let go of a grudge, and, if it's the right thing to do, to reconcile with the person or institution that hurt you.

Nelson Mandela, who before he was elected president of South Africa, spent twenty-seven years in prison for his stance against apartheid. Professor Tammy Lenski, an expert on conflict resolution, shares this story about Bill Clinton and Nelson Mandela:

> Mandela made a grand, elegant, dignified exit from prison and it was very, very powerful for the world to see. But as I watched him walking down that dusty road, I wondered whether he was thinking about the last 27 years, whether he was angry all over again. Later, many years later, I had a chance to ask him. I said, "Come on, you were a great man, you invited your jailers to your inauguration, you put your pressures on the government. But tell me the truth. Weren't you really angry all over again?" And he said, "Yes, I was angry. And I was a little afraid. After all I've not been free in so long. But," he said, "when I felt that anger well up inside of me I realized that if I hated them after I got outside that gate then they would still have me." And he smiled and

said, "I wanted to be free so I let it go." It was an astonishing moment in my life. It changed me.[1]

This freedom is what I want for you. This is a how-to book, a book of how to "let go" and be free, a book of practical spirituality—a spirituality that is both natural and supernatural; natural in that it is rooted in human nature, and supernatural in that it reaches outside of the human for healing.

Think of spirituality as a sixth sense, a sensitivity to a mystery outside yourself. You can't see or adequately define the mystery, but it manifests itself in various experiences: coincidences that surprise you and move your life along in a good way, a sense of well-being that comes when you experience the beauty of nature or allow yourself to be immersed in prayer, or intuitions that come after meditation. Your sixth sense of spirituality allows you to recognize some intelligence and goodness beyond the human mind and will.

You relate to the intelligence and goodness that transcends humanity, who some people choose to call God, through spiritual activities: prayer, chanting, rituals, meditation, and everything from lighting a candle to feeling like you are ready to burst into flames. You seek strength from the transcendent power, you seek guidance from this wisdom beyond yourself, you ask for help in prayer, and you listen for guidance in meditation.

YOUR INNER PRIEST

The traditional role of a priest in any religion is to mediate between the immanent and the transcendent, between the natural world and the supernatural world, between Creator and creation, between the human and the Divine. You have an inner priest who mediates the God experience. Another name for this inner priest is spirituality. This inner priest must be formed in the ways of God so that it can effectively relate to God and mediate between the individual and God. Your spirituality mediates between your whole self and God.

This priest also mediates God in you to the world around you. It presides over how you interact with the world when you seek to make the world holy, that is, whole or at one with God. Your inner priest mediates the divine spark in you with the divine spark in others. Sometimes the connection is easy, but sometimes there is so much corrosion the spark can't jump. Cleaning up the corrosion so the spark can jump is the inner priest's hard work. Forgiveness is a principle way you clean up the corrosion.

Forgiveness is a skill that can be taught and a spirituality to be lived. As with any skill, you start small and work your way up. In the spiritual life, you don't start out as a saint; you begin as a newcomer, a novice; you start with what Eastern spirituality calls a beginner's mind. You are urged on by grace. Christians believe the power of the Holy Spirit, what is also called grace, is what enables you to advance in the spiritual life. The Holy Spirit, the presence of God in your life, or Grace, attracts you to prowl deeper into the mystery of God.

St. John of the Cross, in the Daniel Ladinsky translation, writes:

> The sleeping man is blessed with
> a faith that is not
> active.

> Faith as it ripens turns into an almost insatiable appetite,

> and the awake lion must prowl for God
> in places it once
> feared.[2]

My suggestion to you is to learn forgiveness by starting with a small- to moderate-sized resentment. Think of a resentment that you could practice with; it could be a current one or a grudge from the past. Not a giant hurt. Not the parent who abandoned you. Not the spouse who divorced you. Not the murderer who killed your loved one. Not the lover who broke your heart. Not the person who sexually abused you. You want to work your way up to forgiving big hurts by starting with a small- to medium-sized hurt, something that still grates at you, like not being invited to a wedding, or the girl who said, "I'm just not that into you," or the boss that didn't give you the bonus you know you deserved, or the neighbor who threw trash on your lawn. Use this small hurt as the example to return to as you practice the exercises in this book.

In this book, the process of LET GO (L-E-T G-O) is designed to teach you to be a more forgiving person, to help you make forgiveness a way of life. Once you've become a master of forgiveness, then you can take on the heroic job of forgiving the unforgivable.

Start small and work your way up. Don't take on the tragedies of your life that right now seem unforgivable. Wait until you are ready for those bigger and deeper hurts. Someday you can find the redemption from the crucifixion. For the Christian, nothing is unforgivable because nothing is unredeemable. In the power of Christ's resurrection, you can bring new life out of death, but, just as there was a day between Good Friday and Easter Sunday, you may have to live in Holy Saturday for a time.

Timing is important with forgiveness. After a tragedy, you need to recognize the enormity of what has happened, go through the time of outrage, express your anger, mourn your loss, and honor your grief. When you have just gone through a terrible hurt—such as the murder of a child, betrayal by your spouse, the loss of a home by a fire caused by a careless neighbor—the suggestion immediately that you forgive the malefactor dishonors your grief.

Each person needs to let others go through the shock, rage, and grief that comes with life's most serious blows. After you have experienced the normal course of strong emotions brought on by horrific heartbreaks and are tired of feeling terrible, then the day will come when you feel worn out from these wrung-out emotions, and you will want to stretch your spirit in the sun and move on. That is the day when you can start the process of forgiveness; then you are ready to seek the grace of letting go. Forgiveness is a process. There is no magic, only the spiritual work outlined in this book and the grace of God to help you get through the hurt.

While doing a parish mission in a Midwestern state, a woman told me a story about her daughter. The daughter, a young teacher at the time, was hit by a drunk driver. Eventually, five surgeries put her broken body back together. Two days after the accident, a eucharistic minister from the local parish visited the teacher who lay in a hospital bed. After hearing the young woman's story, the poorly trained minister said, "I won't give you communion until you forgive the man who did this to you."

The young teacher was not in a forgiving mood. She was still in the stage of shock and outrage at what had been done to her. She not only didn't get communion, she wrote off the Church and was finished with God. Much later, a caring priest undid the damage, and the young woman was able to move on with her life. She accepted what the drunk driver did to her, and she forgave the eucharistic minister and has returned as a member of the Church.

It would have been much better if the minister had acknowledged the woman's outrage at the injury inflicted on her and reassured her of God's presence even in the tragedy. With forgiveness, timing is important. You have to pass through the initial feelings of outrage, anger, and grief, and then work through the injustice so that you can move on to a new normal.

CAN YOU LOVE THE WAY GOD LOVES?

Some days the big question is "Can I love the way God loves?" In any given situation, will you make the most loving choice?

The first thing the Bible says about us is that we are made in the image and likeness of God: "Then God said, 'Let us make humankind in our image, according to our likeness'" (Gen 1:26).

Toward the end of the Bible, after we see the evidence of Jesus' life, we are told who God is: God Is Love. "God is love, and those who abide in love abide in God, and God abides in them" (1 John 4:16).

You are made in the image of God, and God is love so you are created to love. So, can you act like God and love? Sometimes love is easy, when you see a baby, especially your own, you can't help but love. When you meet the girl or boy of your dreams and fall in love, love is easy. But what happens when that child grows up and rejects you? What happens when the dream relationship turns into a nightmare? When love is hard, how can you love? God gave you Jesus Christ to show you how to love even in the shadow of the cross. You may not be able to love on your own, but you can let Christ love through you.

Love has been perfected among us in this: that we may have boldness on the day of judgment, because as he is, so are we in this world. There is no fear in love, but perfect love casts out fear; for fear has to do with punishment, and whoever fears has not reached perfection in love. We love because he first loved us. Those who say, "I love God," and hate their brothers or sisters, are liars; for those who do not love a brother or sister whom they have seen, cannot love God whom they have not seen. The commandment we have from him is this: those who love God must love their brothers and sisters also. (1 John 4:17–21)

You are created to be like Jesus, that is, to empty yourself of all that is not love.

> Though he was in the form of God,
>   did not regard equality with God
>   as something to be exploited,
> but emptied himself,
>   taking the form of a slave,
>   being born in human likeness. (Phil 2:6–7a)

FORGIVENESS AS A SPIRITUAL PRACTICE

Forgiveness is a primary way for you to become what we are made to be: "But I say to you, Love your enemies and pray for those who persecute you, so that you may be children of your Father in heaven" (Matt 5:44–45).

Speaking about Rev. Martin Luther King, his fellow founder of the Southern Christian Leadership Conference and lifelong civil rights worker, Rev. Joseph Lowery said, "Part of his basic teaching [was] that we not get bogged down with hate, because then we couldn't be effective instruments of change."[3]

Dr. King learned the lesson that in order to be a child of God, you have to grow in love to where you can even love your enemies. That kind of love is a powerful love, a love that can shift societies.

The power of self-emptying love is recognized not just in Christianity, but is built into human nature. While making the film, I met Dr. George Ellis, a South African astrophysicist and cosmologist. He co-authored a book, *On the Moral Nature of the Universe: Theology, Cosmology and Ethics*. Dr. Ellis and his co-author, theologian Nancey Murphy, make the case that creation is a process of self-emptying, that the original moment of that self-emptying was the Big Bang, and that the universe continues through this process of self-emptying. He makes this argument through a mathematical study of the origin of the universe. This process they name *kenosis* based on the Greek word for empty, *kenosis*. They speculate that this is reflective of the nature of the Creator, which is to say, God is self-emptying love, the Creator has gone out of self to create and continues to extend the Divine Self in creation.

When you forgive, you go out of yourself in love and so you participate in the divine. It was the poet Alexander Pope who said, "To err is human, to forgive divine." It is human to make mistakes, to damage your relationships. On your own, you can't fully forgive. You need God's help. By God's grace, that is, God's Spirit working in you, you are able to extend yourself in love and offer the gift of forgiveness. As you have been forgiven, so you can forgive.

> As God's chosen ones, holy and beloved, clothe yourselves with compassion, kindness, humility, meekness, and patience. Bear with one another and, if anyone has a complaint against another, forgive each other; just as the Lord has forgiven you, so you also must forgive. Above all, clothe

yourselves with love, which binds everything together in perfect harmony. (Col 3:12–14)

Christians are disciples of Christ. That means they follow the discipline offered by Christ to his followers. Forgiveness is a part of the discipline disciples practice. As you practice forgiveness, you get better at being a forgiving person. This is what I've learned, that in order to learn how to forgive, you have to do it. The more you forgive, the better you get at it. The beginning of forgiveness is a gift, a grace. God forgives you and gives you the grace to forgive others. When you avail yourself of that gift and extend it to others, you practice forgiveness. We don't do it perfectly, that's why it's called practice.

NOTES

1. AGENCE FRANCE-PRESSE, "Bill Clinton on forgiveness and Mandela's demon," http://www.rappler.com/world /regions/africa/nelson-mandela/34210-bill-clinton-man dela-tribute-birthday, accessed August 22, 2013.

2. Daniel Ladinsky, *Love Poems from God, Twelve Sacred Voices from the East and the West* (New York: Penguin Compass, 2002).

3. Rev. Joseph Lowery in *The Big Question: A Film about Forgiveness.*

CHAPTER ONE

ARE SOME THINGS UNFORGIVABLE?

It's normal to wonder "Are some things unforgivable?" What should you think about atrocities like the Holocaust, the Armenian genocide, 9/11, the slaughter of the Tutsis in Rwanda? The list could go on and on. A question to ask yourself is how do such atrocities affect you personally? It's one thing to feel outraged against injustice, and it is another thing to be the victim of the injustice. In one case you are a witness to inhumanity; in the other, you personally suffer because of it.

Some monstrosities are none of your business to forgive; they are too big for an individual to forgive. It's none of your business to forgive the Turks for the genocide of the Armenians or the Nazis for the Holocaust or the Hutus for the slaughter of the Tutsis in Rwanda. The only people who can forgive are the ones who have actually been injured by the perpetrator, that is, only Holocaust survivors can forgive the Nazis who put them through hell. Forgiveness is a personal thing. You don't—and can't—do it for someone else.

You may ask, "Isn't it true that what is done to one is done to all? As members of the human race when one person suffers, we all suffer." That is true in a global sense, but the focus of this book is on your individual hurts. The focus here is on you as a spiritual being having human experiences.

Your goal is to grow spiritually through whatever happens in your life. Most people's grievances happen on the domestic stage; your hurts happen within your family, where you work, and within your church, that is to say, in the course of your everyday personal relationships.

Having said this, you may be someone who is personally carrying a resentment rooted in a hurt caused by one of the horrendous malefactions; perhaps you are a family member of a victim of the terrorist attacks of 9/11 or perhaps your parents were Holocaust survivors. My stance, a Christian stance, is that anyone can make personal peace with the hurts of the past even as you recognize the evil of the injustice. Forgiveness is a personal thing. You forgive hurts done to you, first for your own sake and then to help the greater community to be at peace, and, ultimately, because it is how you grow into who you are meant to be: the image of God.

For the Christian, all things are forgivable because all things are redeemable. God's power can make all things new. If God can raise Jesus from the dead and you share in the resurrection of Christ through your faith, then you too can be raised from any death.

As you read in Paul's second letter to the Corinthians, "if anyone is in Christ, there is a new creation: everything old has passed away; see, everything has become new" (2 Cor 5:17).

Nothing is unforgivable if you chose to forgive. You are in control of your attitude toward the offense. Forgiveness means you are no longer in bondage to the event. You can choose to free yourself by giving the gift of forgiveness.

Nothing is unforgivable, but some things are irreconcilable. I believe that you can forgive anything, that is, let go of feelings of resentment, if you are willing and work with

God's grace. God wants you to live in peace with others, but in this imperfect world, there may be reasons you don't reconcile with some people. At the end of the book, I will return to this theme when discussing reconciliation.

You may ask yourself, "What about sociopaths? You don't want to reconcile with someone who has no conscience and is just going to hurt you again." I would say, "Yes, and, also, you have to be careful of anyone who is an addict." Experience shows that helping a sick person to continue to act on an addiction is not love; it is enabling bad behavior. Only tough love helps some people. If the person doesn't want to stop the addiction, then reconciliation with them may not be helpful to them or to you.

WHY SHOULD YOU FORGIVE?

Let's look at some reasons why you should forgive. Forgiveness is good for your body, mind, and spirit. You probably know that intuitively. But there is plenty of research to show that forgiveness improves your physical health. Chronic anger causes the body to release too much cortisol, metacortisol, and adrenaline. A steady flow of these biochemicals puts stress on your system. Stress weakens your immune system and can cause ulcers, heart attacks, and strokes. Practicing forgiveness can lower your blood pressure and heart rate. Forgiveness can help reduce chronic pain.

Dr. Pietro Pietrini, doctor of clinical biochemistry at the University of Pisa, Italy, says forgiving developed over time as a natural defense against the pain of hurts inflicted on us by others.

According to Dr. Pietrini, when subjects forgive, there is a greater activation in the anterior singular cortex, the part of the brain involved in emotional processing. This part of the brain is also involved in perception of pain and in pain relief. He says you can speculate that forgiveness is a sort of sulphate medication that the brain has developed in the course of evolution to take care of its own pain.

In other words, forgiveness is a medication the brain uses to reduce feelings of anger. This self-medication in the brain improves your mental health. Obsessive thinking about a hurt or about revenge just keeps you in the hurt; you re-traumatize yourself as you keep ruminating on what happened and how you want to get back at the other person. You give so much attention to past hurts that you divert your attention from a positive vision of the future. You soak in bitterness and then turn sour.

When you are locked in unforgiveness, you can gradually isolate yourself from friends. Your relationships suffer. Friends ease themselves out of your life because your bitterness is spoiling the relationship. On the other hand, forgiveness improves friendships and your sense of well-being; forgiveness lessens symptoms of depression, anxiety, and hopelessness. With forgiveness, you are restored to a more optimistic outlook on life.

My own experience is that when I forgive someone, that person changes from being a pain-in-the-neck to a person-like-me. The change, of course, is not really in the other person but in me!

Forgiveness improves a person's spiritual health. Every major religion teaches forgiveness as necessary to maintain harmony in human community and to maintain harmony in one's relationship to the Divine. Jesus clearly wanted people to develop forgiveness as a spiritual practice.

FOR CHRISTIANS FORGIVENESS IS NONNEGOTIABLE

Jesus taught his disciples only one prayer. It's short and perfect. It's the prayer Christians pray all the time.

> Our Father in heaven,
> hallowed be your name.
> Your kingdom come.
> Your will be done,
>   on earth as it is in heaven.
> Give us this day our daily bread.
> *And forgive us our debts,*
>   *as we also have forgiven our debtors.*
> And do not bring us to the time of trial,
>   but rescue us from the evil one.
>   (Matt 6:9–13; Luke 11:2–4)

Jesus emphasized the spiritual necessity of forgiveness. When he teaches his disciples the central prayer of Christianity, he immediately comments on only one clause in the prayer, the one about forgiveness: *"For if you forgive others their trespasses, your heavenly Father will also forgive you; but if you do not forgive others, neither will your Father forgive your trespasses"* (Matt 6:14).

In our desire to go easy on ourselves, it is easy to overlook the clarity of the reciprocity: if we want God to forgive us, then we have to forgive. We have to accept God's forgiveness and give it away to others.

The way I interpret Jesus' saying "if you do not forgive, neither will your Father forgive you" is that God's forgiveness is already available to you. In the kingdom of God you are forgiven and forgiveness is the rule. If you don't extend forgiveness to others, than you put yourself outside of God's Kingdom. God doesn't go against your free will; when you make a decision to be unforgiving, you are deciding to renounce the grace available to you.

In the letter to the Colossians, you hear: *"Bear with one another and, if anyone has a complaint against another, forgive each other; just as the Lord has forgiven you, so you also must forgive. Above all, clothe yourselves with love, which binds everything together in perfect harmony"* (Col 3:13–14).

When you know in your heart that you are forgiven by God, then you are able to forgive others from your heart. You are able to forgive because you know what it is to be forgiven.

I love poetry, and I love the poetry of this passage from St. Luke:

"Love your enemies, do good,
and lend, expecting to nothing in return.
Your reward will be great,
and you will be children of the Most High;
for he is kind to the ungrateful and the wicked.
Be merciful, just as your Father is merciful.

"Do not judge, and you will not be judged;
do not condemn, and you will not be condemned.
Forgive, and you will be forgiven;
give, and it will be given to you.
A good measure, pressed down, shaken together,
    running over,
will be put into your lap;
for the measure you give will be the measure
    you get back."

(Luke 6:35–38)

Jesus tells us that not only is there a reciprocity—give a gift and a gift will be given to you—there is also an escalating abundance. God wants you to share the gift of forgiveness and when you do God pours out even more kindness upon you. When you spread forgiveness around, you find yourself surrounded by it. You lay the foundation for a community of people to grow up around you that will extend back to you and to each other in understanding and compassion. This is what it is to build the kingdom of God.

Even if others do not give back to you or pay forward to others the gift you give to them, you know that you are becoming more and more like your Creator. If others choose not to extend the reign of God in the world, you have helped to build the reign of God in your heart.

THE UNFORGIVING SERVANT

The Parable of the Unforgiving Servant found in St. Matthew's Gospel looks at how Jesus spoke of God's forgiveness and our forgiveness:

> Then Peter came and said to him, "Lord, if another member of the church sins against me, how often should I forgive? As many as seven times?" Jesus said to him, "Not seven times, but, I tell you, seventy-seven times.
>
> "For this reason the kingdom of heaven may be compared to a king who wished to settle accounts with his slaves. When he began the reckoning, one who owed him ten thousand talents was brought to him; and, as he could not pay, his lord ordered him to be sold, together with his wife and children and all his possessions, and payment to be made. So the slave fell on his knees before him, saying,

'Have patience with me, and I will pay you everything.' And out of pity for him, the lord of that slave
released him and forgave him the debt. But that
same slave, as he went out, came upon one of his fellow slaves who owed him a hundred denarii; and
seizing him by the throat, he said, 'Pay what you
owe.' Then his fellow slave fell down and pleaded
with him, 'Have patience with me, and I will pay
you.' But he refused; then he went and threw him
into prison until he would pay the debt. When his
fellow slaves saw what had happened, they were
greatly distressed, and they went and reported to
their lord all that had taken place. Then his lord
summoned him and said to him, 'You wicked slave!
I forgave you all that debt because you pleaded with
me. Should you not have had mercy on your fellow
slave, as I had mercy on you?' And in anger his lord
handed him over to be tortured until he would pay
his entire debt. So my heavenly Father will also do
to every one of you, if you do not forgive your
brother or sister from your heart." (Matt 18:21–35)

When Jesus says seven times seventy, he's not talking
literally about us forgiving as many as seventy-seven times.
Peter made the mistake of thinking that there is a limit to
how much we are to forgive. Peter isn't the only one.

There is a story about Hillary Clinton after her husband
was publicly humiliated for being unfaithful to her. A
reporter asked her about this Bible passage. Her response
was, "In the Bible it says they asked Jesus how many times
you should forgive, and he said seventy times seven. Well, I
want you all to know that I'm keeping a chart." I guess this
politician figured she had seventy-seven forgiveness chits to
give out, and when they were exhausted she could switch to

revenge. What Jesus is saying is that such a list will extend forever. Jesus is talking about an infinite number of times we are to forgive. Then he follows up with the story of the forgiven and unforgiving servant.

First, to better understand this parable, know that a denarius was a day's wages for a day laborer. A talent was a thousand denarii. So the first servant owed the master ten million denarii. The second servant owed a hundred denarii. To get a sense of the proportion, it is as if the first slave owed $500,000,000 and the second slave owed $500.

The first servant's debt was so big he could never pay it back. He and his household, that is, his family and possessions, were all to be sold into slavery and whatever profit was made would go toward paying the debt. The master was trying to cut his losses. It was the equivalent of declaring his servant bankrupt and getting a fraction of a cent on the dollar.

The servant begged for more time to pay it back. The master knew the servant was never going to be able to raise that kind of money, so the master gave him more than just an extension of time: his master forgave his servant the entire debt. The master showed mercy. The servant didn't deserve to have the debt forgiven, but his master forgave him—gave him a gift. In giving the servant this gift, it is as if the master wrapped forgiveness around the servant. The master empowered the servant to forgive by showing him real forgiveness. But the servant doesn't use the gift he was given. When he was asked to forgive a much, much smaller debt, the servant said no.

The point of the parable is that God forgives us a debt we could never pay, and he empowers us to extend that forgiveness to others. That's what it means to live in the kingdom of God, to live under the reign of God. Forgiveness is part of the package. It's what is expected of us. God gave us the power, and when we don't use it, we are impeding the growth of the kingdom and cutting God out of our lives. When we don't forgive, we are putting ourselves outside the reign of God. God wants everyone to live under his reign, to live in his kingdom, to help build his kingdom, and when we put ourselves outside the kingdom by choosing not to forgive, God respects our choice.

By choosing not to forgive, the first servant goes to a debtors' prison, where he is continually tortured until he pays the money back. If he or his family can't pay the debt, then he is forever tortured. That sounds like hell to me. When we don't forgive, we are choosing to put ourselves in hell. We choose to live in an emotional debtors' prison where we are tortured by feelings of anger, resentment, and the unsatisfied desire for revenge. We can put ourselves in prison, or we can forgive and live in the kingdom of God.

The Sermon on the Mount provides much to reflect upon:

> Blessed are the merciful, for they will receive mercy. (Matt 5:7)

> Do not judge, so that you may not be judged. For with the judgment you make you will be judged, and the measure you give will be the measure you get. Why do you see the speck in your neighbor's eye, but do not notice the log in your own eye? Or how can you say to your neighbor, "Let me take the speck out of your eye," while the log is in your own eye? You hypocrite, first take the log out of your own eye, and then you will see clearly to take the speck out of your neighbor's eye. (Matt 7:1–5)

> But I say to you, Love your enemies and pray for those who persecute you. (Matt 5:44)

CHAPTER TWO

WHAT FORGIVENESS IS AND WHAT FORGIVENESS IS NOT

Before looking in depth at forgiveness, you should survey the landscape of your current understanding of forgiveness with this True/False quiz. Take this test then look at my take on the test on the following pages.

QUIZ TO GAUGE YOUR UNDERSTANDING OF FORGIVENESS

1. When you are trying to forgive, you must give up being angry. True/False
2. When you forgive, you forget. True/False
3. To forgive means letting the person back into your life and hitting the reset button. True/False
4. Forgiveness is putting up with abusive behavior. True/False
5. You should wait until the person who hurt you apologizes before you forgive. True/False
6. Forgiveness says "That's okay" when the person gives a reason for hurting you. True/False
7. Forgiveness means confronting the person who hurt you with your anger and telling her how her behavior hurt you. True/False

8. Forgiveness is deciding to not get even with the person who hurt you. True/False
9. Forgiveness is accepting the person, warts and all. True/False
10. It is good to tell the story of what happened to you over and over in order to vent your anger. True/False
11. Forgiveness is letting go of hard feelings and thoughts of revenge. True/False
12. Forgiveness is a one-time event; I forgive and move on. True/False[1]

QUIZ REVIEW

1. *When you are trying to forgive, you must give up being angry.* **False.** Anger is a necessary emotion in the forgiveness process. When someone betrays you, you lose something. You lose your trust for the person, you lose the relationship as it was, and you lose a sense of security. All these losses trigger feelings of anger and sadness. Some people feel the anger and their sadness is not so apparent; it could be hidden under the anger. Some people feel the sadness, but the anger it not so apparent. It is necessary to pass through these feelings to get to forgiveness. If you are sad, you have to grieve the losses and then move through the feelings to the other side. If you get stuck in the sadness, you just get depressed. If you are angry, you have to acknowledge the anger and find ways to move through it. If you get stuck in the anger, you just get bitter.

Forgiveness passes through grief and anger to get to peace.

2. *When you forgive, you forget.* **False.** Maybe God can forgive and forget (see Jer 31:34), but we can't and shouldn't. The old adage "forgive and forget" works for slight hurts but not for significant transgressions. The fact is we may not be able to forget. A memory is formed, especially if it was a life-changing hurt inflicted on us. The memory may change over time, the pain may diminish and with forgiveness even disappear, but you can't forget what happened. Trying to forget the memory can make it worse; it becomes more persistent. As Archbishop Desmond Tutu says, we should forgive and remember; in the film he says, "Look the beast in the eye." We want to remember the hurt so that we know the value of the forgiveness. We want to remember the transgression so we can guard against it happening again.

3. *To forgive means letting the person back into your life and hitting the reset button.* **False.** Forgiving a person doesn't mean you have to stay in relationship with the person. You can forgive but not reconcile with the person, especially if there is evidence that the person will repeat an unacceptable, hurtful behavior. Forgiving and staying in relationship with the person, as Rabbi Doff points out in the film, are two separate decisions. You and the other person can agree to start over again, and this may smooth out the relationship, but it doesn't mean that forgiveness has happened. You may just be practicing a form of denial, acting like the hurt didn't happen. You

may be signaling to the person who hurt you that it doesn't matter to you that you were hurt. This just opens the door for this person to hurt you again. The true value of the forgiveness is based on the depth of the hurt: the deeper the hurt, the more valuable the forgiveness. You don't want your forgiveness to be cheap. It doesn't work to suppress the feelings of hurt or anger; they will keep coming back until you deal with them in a positive way, such as the path of forgiveness.

4. *Forgiveness is putting up with abusive behavior.* **False.** Tolerating hurtful behavior is not forgiveness; it's more like masochism. You will probably continue to resent the person, and your anger toward the person will never really diminish as with true forgiveness.

5. *You should wait until the person who hurt you apologizes before you forgive.* **False.** You could wait your whole life, never get an apology, and thus never be free from your resentment. When you are waiting for an apology, you feel that the person owes you something and that you are waiting for them to pay up. If they never apologize, you never have the satisfaction of having the debt repaid. There are two kinds of forgiveness: conditional forgiveness and unconditional forgiveness. Conditional forgiveness is based on the condition of an apology. If the apology doesn't come, then forgiveness is not given. Unconditional forgiveness doesn't wait for an apology. It cancels the debt so that the person doing the forgiving can move on with his or her life. You may ask, "Shouldn't I make the person apologize so

that we can move on?" Forcing a person to apologize to you so that you can continue the relationship doesn't work; the other person has to come to a sense of regret and apologize on his or her own. Forcing an apology may make *you* feel better, that justice has been done, but it may also just make the other person more resentful and keep the cycle of hurt and revenge whirling around.

6. *Forgiveness says "That's okay" when the person gives a reason for hurting you.* **False.** You can accept a person's excuse, that is, acceptance of a reality, but it is not forgiveness. Forgiveness is a decision you make to extend a gift to the other person. You can accept the person's valid explanation for what went wrong between you, but that doesn't mean that you have forgiven the person for hurting you. You have to be careful that you don't accept an excuse that is a lie because then the other person will think he or she can hurt you again with impunity, that you are a pushover, and that the door is open for you to be reinjured.

7. *Forgiveness means confronting the person with your anger and telling her how her behavior hurt you.* **False.** This is more like picking a fight than forgiveness. It may be a good idea to have a heart-to-heart talk with the person who hurt you when it is just a conversation, an approach at good communication. If the approach to the other person is done with honesty and goodwill, then you may go a long way on the road to forgiveness. A confrontation, however, may not help. Blaming the person for what she did wrong

is not forgiveness. It is getting in her face and making sure the hurt stays in the forefront of your relationship. When the other person senses your contempt for her, then you lose your moral power to persuade her to see things from your perspective. Confrontation done in anger will just inspire more resentment and fuel a cycle of retaliation.

8. *Forgiveness is deciding to not get even with the person who hurt you.* **True.** Putting away revenge thoughts is a mark of decisional forgiveness. You decide you forgive the person, and you prove it by restraining any action against the person. (Later in the book, you'll see the difference between decisional and emotional forgiveness and how to get from one to the other.) This is true forgiveness because it tells the truth. A wrong has been done to you and you acknowledge that you have been hurt; you say, "Ouch!" Even though you have been hurt, you have chosen not to seek revenge and not to condemn the person who hurt you. You do not speak ill of the person to others.

9. *Forgiveness is accepting the person, warts and all.* **False.** Accepting someone warts and all is just that, acceptance. It's not the same as forgiveness. You can see the person's flaws and accept that the person has those flaws and may never change. That does not mean you condone the person's behavior or that you forgive him or her for it. You can accept someone as a bully, the person is who he is and probably won't change; you don't have to like that he is a bully or let him bully you.

10. *It is good to tell the story of what happened to you over and over in order to vent your anger.* **False.** Psychoanalyst Sigmund Freud advocated getting in touch with anger and expressing it. This catharsis was intended to relieve anger and can be helpful in uncovering suppressed anger or taking the edge off a recent anger. More recent psychological theory, however, says that telling the same story over and over again and getting worked up about the injustice keep the hurt alive. It's like picking at a scab and not letting a wound heal. When I tell the story of my hurt over and over again, I get trapped as a victim in my own story. Getting angry all over again doesn't relieve anger; it just keeps it alive and makes it worse. You turn your one-time anger into chronic anger and trigger all the poor health effects associated with such bitterness. Telling the story over and over again carves a rut in your brain, and a rut is just a narrow grave. You climb down into your victim story and can't get out.

11. *Forgiveness is letting go of hard feelings and thoughts of revenge.* **True.** This is true forgiveness. You make a decision to not seek revenge and decide to behave in such a way as to keep the transgression in the past. This allows your relationship with the other person to go forward, if you both choose to do so. It clears the stage so that your emotional scenery can be changed. Emotional forgiveness happens when your feelings toward the person change from negative to at least a neutral feeling like understanding or a positive feeling such as empathy.

12. *Forgiveness is a one-time event; I forgive and move on.* **False.** Forgiveness is an ongoing process, a way of life. Even after you decide to forgive someone and your feelings about that person change, some event may trigger a reappearance of resentment, fear, or grief. This doesn't mean you didn't forgive, it means you must go deeper into the process of forgiveness. You must work through the newly revealed feelings as you move forward as a forgiving person.

WHAT FORGIVENESS IS NOT

In summary, we can say what forgiveness is not:

Forgiveness is not condoning bad behavior. "Let anyone among you who is without sin be the first to throw a stone at her" (John 8:7). Jesus never condoned sin, but he forgave the sinner as in the story of the woman caught in adultery in the Gospel of John. Forgiveness doesn't pretend as if bad behavior didn't occur. It acknowledges the bad behavior and chooses to forgive the person who did the harm. Forgiveness is a way of doing the truth in charity. You tell the truth about the hurt, you express charity by giving the person the gift of forgiveness.

Forgiveness is not bypassing justice. Forgiveness does not mean you dispense with the process of working for justice. Some say forgiveness moves people prematurely to accept a situation that needs to be challenged, such as a wife who enables an alcoholic spouse by covering for him with his boss. That's not forgiveness; that's appeasement. It's going along to get along. Forgiveness is not a cheap way to get out of a difficult situation. You may very well have to stand up to injustice, to confront bad behavior, not condone it.

Heroic forgivers like Mahatma Gandhi, Dr. Martin Luther King, and Archbishop Desmond Tutu confronted injustice and practiced forgiveness simultaneously. They followed Jesus' injunction to meet evil with good as found in Paul's Letter to the Romans:

> Do not repay anyone evil for evil, but take thought for what is noble in the sight of all. If it is possible, so far as it depends on you, live at peaceably with all. Beloved, never avenge yourselves, but leave room for the wrath of God; for it is written, "Vengeance is mine, I will repay, says the Lord." No, "if your enemies are hungry, feed them; if they are thirsty, give them something to drink; for by doing this you will heap burning coals on their heads." Do not be overcome by evil, but overcome evil with good. (Rom 12:17–21)

Forgiveness is not forgetting. Forgetting the injustice, the harm, is dangerous. You want to remember the past so that you are not doomed to repeat it. This is why remembrance of the Holocaust is so important to Jews. They not only want to remember the dead to honor them, but also to remember what happens when anti-Semitism or any sort of racism is allowed to take hold and take action.

The same is true in your personal relationships. You want to remember the mistakes you have made, the ways people have mistreated you so you can be on your guard. You want to protect yourself but keeping a lookout is not the same as building a wall. You want to continue to be open to new experiences and intimate relationships even though you will be vulnerable to hurts. This is why learning the skills of forgiveness is so important.

It is also important to remember the hurt so that you know the value of the forgiveness. The value of the forgiveness you give is in relation to the amount of harm done to you: big hurt = big forgiveness. If you minimize the extent of the hurt done to you, then you devalue the gift of forgiveness that you give.

Forgiveness is not giving in. Forgiveness is not capitulation or appeasement. It's not going along to get along. Saying "No problem" becomes a problem when there really is a problem. Forgiveness does not mean you are giving your power away to the person who hurt you. You can let the person know he was wrong in what he did, you can express your hurt, and then you can give the gift of forgiveness. If you look someone in the eye and say you don't want to be hurt again and then give that person the gift of forgiveness, you are coming from a position of strength, not weakness.

"But speaking the truth in love, we must grow up in every way into him who is the head, into Christ" (Eph 4:15). You want to speak the truth, but you want to speak the truth with love. Truth without love is brutality, which is another way of saying what St. Catherine of Siena wrote to Pope Urban VI: "Were justice without mercy, it would abide in the shadows of cruelty." This has come down to us in the more colloquial form: "Say what you mean. Mean what you say. But don't say it mean." You have to tell the truth but not use the truth to try to hurt people. Everyone has traits or actions they are not proud of and don't want to have rubbed in their face. You tell the truth to help people, not to hurt them.

Forgiveness is not reconciliation. Forgiveness is a one-way street you go down to move past your hurts, resentments, and thoughts of revenge. The street may lead you away from the person who hurt you. Reconciliation is a two-way street; the other person has to come to meet you at least half way. Reconciliation is restoring the relationship so that you can pick up where you left off before the offense that broke the relationship. As Rabbi Dorff points out, you may not want to reconcile with the person who hurt you, you may not want to open the door to be reinjured. The other person may not want to reconcile with you. You *don't* need an apology to forgive someone. You *do* need an apology to reconcile with someone. In order for reconciliation to happen, there has to be some remorse for the hurt and a willingness to make some sort of restitution. You will learn more about reconciliation later in the book.

WHAT FORGIVENESS IS

We forgive to let go of H-A-R-M:

Hurt—the pain and sadness you carry that leads to
Anger—the wrathful sort, that builds up in you and
leads to
Resentment—which can fuel obsessive revenge
thoughts and
Malice—a meanness of spirit that starts aimed at the
person but poisons your spirit and seeps into your
other relationships.

Forgiveness is a decision. You decide to let go your
resentments and thoughts of revenge. You decide to cancel
the emotional debt the other person owes you. You do this to
free yourself from destructive feelings. You forgive a person,
situation, or institution that hurt you to save yourself from
being eaten alive with anger, from poisoning your soul with
resentment. You forgive yourself to save yourself from being
plagued by feelings of shame and guilt.

You may think, "I'm not being eaten alive by anger, my
soul isn't poisoned by resentment." I too may think that
many days I'm not aware of any anger, but then I'll take time
to meditate and realize that there is something bothering
me. Sometimes it's something huge—a mistake that I have to
live with. Or it may be something small, like a friend's annoy-
ing habit. Even small things can erode my spiritual well-
being. Forgiveness is good spiritual medicine for big or small
resentments.

For a religious person, forgiveness is a decision to
accept God's grace of forgiveness and extend it to others. You
let go of the other person's sin against you, and show the
same mercy that God has shown you. You let go of the hurts

you've caused yourself. You forgive yourself for the hurts you've caused others so that you can release the guilt of some long-standing memory.

The decision to forgive, decisional forgiveness, opens you up to working through the process of forgiveness to get to emotional forgiveness. Eventually, as you work through the steps of forgiveness you will start to feel different toward the other person or feel differently toward yourself, if the person you need to forgive is you. You will know you have achieved emotional forgiveness when your feelings change, when you no longer feel hurt, anger, or grief because of the injury to you. You will know you have forgiven when you can pray for the person rather than plan how to get back at him or her.

Forgiveness is difficult, especially for big transgressions that you may not be able to forgive on your own. You need God's power to help you to do what you can't do on your own. This leads to another big question, "How do we let go?"

NOTES

1. The idea for this quiz comes from Dr. Everett Worthington. He uses it in the class he teaches on forgiveness.

CHAPTER THREE

THE FIVE STEPS
OF FORGIVENESS:
HOW DO YOU LET GO?

When you are wrestling with resentment, it's hard to get free. It's easy to say, "Just let it go," but practically, how do you let go?

A simple process that follows five steps can help you let go of hurt and resentment. These are simple steps but not shortcuts and it may take some time to step past a big resentment and see it over your shoulder.

The five steps that lead you along the path of forgiveness were developed during the time I was making *The Big Question: A Film About Forgiveness*. One of the men featured in the film, Dr. Everett Worthington, showed me the way to this path of forgiveness. A preeminent teacher and researcher of forgiveness, he taught me a process of letting go and then told me how it worked in his own life.

The Five Steps of Forgiveness are set up in the acrostic L-E-T G-O. I've found that this five-step process helps me to forgive individual transgressions, and when practiced as a spiritual discipline, it has helped me to become a more forgiving, compassionate person. When I forgive, I feel closer to God; I feel like I'm more of who I was made to be.

The five steps of letting go of a grudge are:

Look deeply at what went wrong.
Empathy is the key.
Tell the story differently.
Give forgiveness freely.
One day at a time, keep forgiveness strong.

As you make your way through these steps, keep in mind what we hear in the Gospel of Luke: "Do not fear. Only believe" (8:50). Your work is to stay open in prayer, and it is God's part to lead you step by step along the way to a new freedom.

PARALLELS FOR THE FIVE STEPS

This wisdom of letting go is universal. It's a part of being human. There are many expressions of it. Some parallels to these five steps include:

T'shuva

The Jewish teaching of *T'shuva*, the Hebrew word for "return," refers to how to restore a broken relationship. In Jewish thought there is no cheap forgiveness; the person who hurt you has to earn your forgiveness. *T'shuva* is the process that you have to go through if you have hurt someone and want that person to forgive you and reconcile with you.

The purpose of forgiveness in the Jewish tradition is to restore your relationship with the person and God; the goal is reconciliation. *T'shuva* is the process of how you restore the relationship. It is an ancient model of restorative justice.

The process of *T'shuva* can be seen in six steps all beginning with "R":

Step 1: Regret. Regret refers to an immediate feeling of sorrow or guilt for what you did.

Rebuilding a relationship starts by acknowledging that you have done something wrong. You regret having hurt another person. The reasonable guilt you feel for hurting another human being is the beginning point for seeking forgiveness.

In order to ask for forgiveness and reconcile, you have to have some grasp of your common humanity with the person whom you have hurt. You need to understand the pain that you inflicted on the person and feel sorry that you caused that pain. You also regret having transgressed God's law of love. This leads you to the second stage of *T'shuva*.

Step 2: Repentance. The process of *T'shuva* is not just about restoring a broken human relationship, it is primarily about returning to God. When you hurt another human being, you have also sinned against God because you have ruptured the love of God.

There is a story in the Gospels where a scholar of the Jewish law wanted to test Jesus and asked him what was the primary commandment of God (Luke 10:25–28). Jesus turned the tables on him and asked, "What is written in the law?" The man replied, "You shall love the Lord your God with all your heart, and with all your soul, and with all your strength, and with all your mind; and your neighbor as yourself." Jesus affirmed the man's answer.

If you love God and love your neighbor, then you can return to God who is your source of life. Your whole life is about returning to God. When you recognize that you have sinned against God and feel remorse, this leads you to repentance. You come to a willingness that you don't want to repeat the hurtful behavior, and you repent your wrongdoing. You resolve that you don't want to be the kind of person who exhibits hurtful behavior. Repentance carries a willing-ness to change, to let go of your faults, and to ask God to replace those faults with virtues. If you slander someone, you ask God to remove the fault of malicious gossip and replace it with affirming speech, as told in Ephesians 4:29: "Let no evil talk come out of your mouths, but only what is useful for building up, as there is need, so that your words may give grace to those who hear."

Being an inconsistent human being, you may relapse into bad behavior, but repentance is the willingness to change your behavior, to resolve to be better.

Step 3: Request for forgiveness. You apologize. With an apology you bring your inner life into the outer world. You tell the other person that you are sorry for your bad behavior, for hurting him or her. You make your intention to be a better person effective by telling the person that you have harmed of your change of heart. You let him know that you don't want to do any more harm to him. You want him to know that you are different. This is how you begin to rebuild trust between you and the person you have hurt.

With apologies, apply the K.I.S.S. principle: keep it sim-ple, supplicant. Let the person know that you understand that you hurt her. When she knows that you have some understanding of how you hurt her feelings or her bank account or her reputation, then it is easier for her to forgive you because she feels understood.

Put yourself in her shoes and from her point of view describe your behavior, and let her know that you under-stand how you hurt her and how it affected her. Then tell her that you are sorry. Express your resolution not to hurt her again. Ask for her forgiveness. Don't burden your apology with elaborate explanations of your behavior or excuses, or foist off on others the blame for your behavior. In its simplest form, your apology should be "I'm sorry I hurt you. I understand how you feel. Please forgive me."

That is the gold standard of apologies. How do most people apologize? There are lots of different ways to apologize. Depending on your sincerity and the other person's mercy, the bar on an apology that works can be lowered. With some people, and I'm thinking of men I know, an apology sometimes is just "Hey, you know the other day when I said that thing. That didn't bother you, did it?" It's not really an apology, it's an acknowledgment that maybe the speaker did something wrong. Between two friends, however, this might be enough.

In a certain village in Bohemia, there was a custom that the week after Easter, when the spring thaw had set in and the roads were passable again and everyone was celebrating, families would host open houses. They would put out food and visit with each other. If two people had a grievance during the year, this was the time when they would repair their relationship. One of the feuding parties would go to the house of the other. If the other welcomed him in, the one shook the other's hand and offered him food and then the reconciliation happened. No words needed to be said; it was enough that one showed up and the other offered hospitality.

There may be times when it's better not to apologize to a person. If the apology is going to do more harm than good, then why do it? If you are apologizing just to clear your conscience but the net effect is going to be that you hurt the other person, then it is better to express your regret to a third person. For example, if the person doesn't know about the harm and revealing it to her is going to injure her, then you're just going to do more harm and you'll end up apologizing for your apology.

A priest, now deceased, represented in his too abundant flesh what I much feared: that I would wind up using food and alcohol to distract myself from loneliness; that someday I would be old, fat, drunk, and maudlin. Until I could articulate this and accept that he was who he was and I didn't have to be him, I avoided him; I held him at a distance with a silent contempt.

When I realized that I was afraid of becoming him, that it was my own fear that was causing me to treat him badly, then I was able to turn my behavior around. I stopped avoiding him and started to listen more and judge less. I changed my behavior, became friendlier, and tried to learn a thing or two from his experience as a priest. We got along much better. It would have been pointless and hurtful for me to come to him and say, "Jack, I'm sorry I avoided you and held you in contempt because I was afraid of becoming you."

The more difficult case is that of the man who has an affair, repents of it, returns to fidelity, and his wife never finds out about it. Should he tell her? Isn't it dishonest to not tell her? Isn't it a further breach of trust to keep the secret from her? Perhaps it is wrong to keep it from her, or perhaps it is the lesser of two wrongs. It may be worse to tell her and have their marriage put in jeopardy. The general rule is honesty and a desire to help the other person. Each case must be decided on what its net effect will be.

Step 4: Restitution. After you apologize, you need to show that you mean it by offering to make right the wrong you have done. To show that you are serious about wanting to restore the relationship, you compensate the person you hurt as best you can for the harm done. If you owe him money, then you pay it back. If you hurt her reputation, you go to the people you gossiped to and take back what you said about her. If you insulted him, then you take back the insult and affirm what is positive about him. You do what is necessary to make the relationship right again. Restitution is necessary to make your relationship with the other person whole again. Restitution allows the other person to start to rebuild trust with you. Restitution is a concrete, practical way of showing that you are actually changing your behavior. The sustained change of behavior over time is what we call rehabilitation.

Step 5: Rehabilitation. The next stage of *T'shuva* is rebuilding the relationship. To rebuild a relationship means that you are reestablishing trust. You have to prove your change of heart by changing your behavior. You show by your actions that you have changed. When you are in a similar situation to the one that got you into trouble the first time, then you act differently.

For example, the transgression may occur when you attend a party with your spouse and you have a few drinks and tell jokes at his or her expense. *T'shuva* demands that the next time you attend a party, you don't humiliate your spouse. Rehabilitation demonstrates a reversal of behavior. When all of these conditions have been met, then the other person can trust enough to come back into relationship.

Step 6: Reconciliation. Reconciliation is the restoration of the broken relationship.

Once you have gone through this process from remorse to changed behavior, then you have laid the foundation so that the other person can rebuild the trust that was broken between you. You have cleared the way for him to enter back into relationship with you. Perhaps there will still be some wariness to be worked through as you continue to build trust. Perhaps you will be back to an even keel with each other, and perhaps the process of restoration will make your relationship stronger.

But if the other person doesn't forgive you, then another

"R" comes into play. You bring in Reinforcements. If the person doesn't forgive you, you need to bring in mutual friends to help mediate between you. You ask friends who are more objective and can help the two of you work out a sincere reconciliation.

Two passages in Scripture show how Jesus reflects this idea. Again, *T'shuva* means return—a return to God and restoration, that is, the restoration of a relationship. In this passage we see that in order to return to God we have to reconcile our relationships.

> You have heard that it was said to those of ancient times, "You shall not murder"; and "whoever murders shall be liable to judgment." But I say to you that if you are angry with a brother or sister, you will be liable to judgment; and if you insult a brother or sister, you will be liable to the council; and if you say, "You fool," you will be liable to the hell of fire. So when you are offering your gift at the altar, if you remember that your brother or sister has something against you, leave your gift there before the altar and go; first be reconciled to your brother or sister, and then come and offer your gift. Come to terms quickly with your accuser while you are on the way to court with him, or your accuser may hand you over to the judge, and the judge to the guard, and you will be thrown into prison. Truly I tell you, you will never get out until you have paid the last penny. (Matt 5:21–26)

In this next passage from Matthew, Jesus tells about the responsibility to approach someone who is doing something to hurt you and to tell him or her how the behavior is affecting you. You are to correct the person, not from a stance of egotism—saying you are right and he or she is wrong—but from the stance that for the good of the relationship with God they don't want to be hurting you or anyone else.

> If another member of the church sins against you, go and point out the fault when the two of you are alone. If the member listens to you, you have regained that one. But if you are not listened to, take one or two others along with you, so that every word may be confirmed by the evidence of two or three witnesses. If the member refuses to listen to them, tell it to the church; and if the offender refuses to listen even to the church, let such a one be to you as a Gentile and a tax collector. (Matt 18:15–17)

This passage introduces the idea of bringing in a friend, reinforcements, to help convince the person that their behavior is not helping further good relationships.

If the person doesn't want to change her behavior toward you, then you are to bring friends of that person with you and ask the person again to stop harming you. The wisdom here is to appeal to the community that is also affected by the breach in your relationship. None of us lives in isolation; we are all members of larger communities that are affected by estrangements.

Mutual friends can be objective about what happened, can see the total effect of the breach, and can argue more dispassionately for a healing of the hurt.

What if the person doesn't forgive you?

In *T'shuva* the same principle of bringing in friends to argue for forgiveness applies. If you have gone through all the steps of *T'shuva* and the person still does not forgive you, then you are to bring in mutual friends to mediate on your behalf. If the person won't listen to your mutual friends, then your last recourse is to bring in a religious authority. If the person still won't forgive you after you have asked a total of three times, then, according to Jewish teaching, you are absolved of your transgression and the person is now guilty of the sin of unforgiveness. You have done what you could, and your relationship with God is restored. If you can't convince the person to forgive you or you can't convince the person that his behavior is hurting you, and if friends or even the Church can't convince the person, then you are to let go with love.

As you can see, *T'shuva* sets the bar high for reconciliation. When you have hurt someone and broken your relationship, you must work hard to restore the relationship. Most of us don't like doing that. The late Trappist monk-mystic-poet Thomas Merton speaks of this in his book *New Seeds of Contemplation*:

> As long as we are on earth, the love that unites us will bring us suffering by our very contact with one another, because this love is the resetting of a Body of broken bones. Even the saints cannot live with saints on this earth without some anguish, without some pain at the differences that come between them. There are two things which men can do about the pain of disunion with other men. They can love or they can hate. Hatred recoils from the sacrifice and the sorrow that are the price of this resetting of bones. It refuses the pain of reunion....But love, by the acceptance of the pain of reunion, begins to heal all wounds.[1]

Sacrament of Reconciliation

Catholics may very well recognize in *T'shuva* a parallel in the sacrament of reconciliation. Sometimes Catholics refer to this sacrament as confession or penance. Both confession and penance are stages within the overall sacrament of reconciliation. The sacrament of reconciliation parallels the six stages of *T'Shuva*. If you stop and think, there are also six distinct stages of the sacrament of reconciliation.

In *T'shuva* the first stage is regret or remorse, recognizing that you have done something wrong, that you have hurt someone, that you have sinned against God. In the sacrament of reconciliation the first step is an **examination of conscience**, a review of your life to see where you feel guilty about an offense against God and neighbor.

The second stage of *T'shuva*, repentance, is the parallel for what Catholics call a **firm purpose of amendment** in the sacrament of reconciliation is; you repent of the wrong you have done and decide to change your behavior.

In *T'shuva* the third step is to request forgiveness, to apologize. In the sacrament of reconciliation you **confess** your sins to a priest and request forgiveness. Some Catholics will end their confession of sins by saying something like, "I ask forgiveness of you and God for these sins and any others I may have committed."

The fourth stage of *T'shuva* is restitution. In the sacrament of reconciliation Catholics do **penance**. The repentant sinners show that they are sorry for their sins by doing some action. Most often it is saying prayers to God. Sometimes a more direct penance is called for. I recall an occasion when a man confessed having a fight with his wife. I asked him if he apologized. He gave me a half-hearted answer. I told him for his penance he should take his wife out to dinner.

One of the reasons Catholics don't utilize the sacrament of reconciliation more often is because they don't see their behavior changing, and they are ashamed of confessing the same things over and over. Perhaps if Catholics took penance more seriously, that is, to make a real restitution to persons harmed, it would motivate people to change their behavior.

The fifth step of *T'shuva* is rehabilitation. In the sacrament of reconciliation the person prays the **Act of Contrition** and the priest offers the prayer of absolution. The person admits to wrongdoing and asks for God's help to behave better. Then the priest says the prayer of absolution and the person is absolved of guilt and offered pardon and the peace of God. In this exchange the person's relationship with God is rehabilitated; they are changed for the good.

The final step of *T'shuva* is restoration or reconciliation. In the sacrament of reconciliation the person is told to **"Go in peace."** They are freed from their sins and are reconciled to God.

To review, here are the six steps of *T'shuva* and the sacrament of reconciliation:

1. Regret/Examination of Conscience
2. Repentance/A Firm Purpose of Amendment
3. Request for Forgiveness/Confession
4. Restitution/Penance
5. Rehabilitation/Contrition and Absolution
6. Reconciliation/Go in Peace

These six steps also provide a reliable and effective model for restoring any broken human relationship.

First, you look deeply at what went wrong; you examine your conscience. When you know what your part in the problem is, then you can tell the other person, confess it to them. You express sorrow for hurting the person and also admit a firm purpose to amend your behavior so you don't hurt that person again. You say, "I'm really sorry I hurt you. I wasn't thinking straight. I never want to do that to you again."

You apologize, which is a confession of what you did wrong and also contains your act of contrition. Any sincere apology should also contain an offer to make amends for the hurt suffered by the other person. "Doing penance" is like making restitution for what you did wrong. In most instances, a person does penance by saying some prayers. The prayers are an action by which you reach out for help and demonstrate that you want to change your behavior.

Penance, to be truly effective in the restoration of a human relationship, involves restitution. You have to say "I'm sorry" with more than your mouth. You may need to get your checkbook involved. If you are guilty because you abused your cat when you were thirteen years old, perhaps an appropriate penance would be to send a check to an organization pledged to protect animals. If you've had a fight with a friend, you need to apologize and perhaps present the friend with a gift as a peace offering.

If the other person forgives you, then you have received your absolution, and if both parties choose, both can be reconciled. If you or the other person chooses not to be reconciled, then you can still go in peace because you have taken responsibility for your actions. If reconciliation happens, then the relationship is restored, and you can return to the relationship healed of the breach.

OTHER PARALLELS TO THE FIVE STEPS OF FORGIVENESS

There are other parallels to the five steps of forgiveness. Those familiar with the **Twelve Steps of Alcoholics Anonymous** may recognize the parallels between the process of *T'shuva* and the sacrament of reconciliation and AA's Steps Four though Nine.

I also am indebted to Dr. Everett Worthington of Virginia Commonwealth University, who taught me his model of forgiveness, which he describes with the acrostic of REACH:

Recall the hurt.
Empathize.
Altruistic gift of forgiveness.
Commit publicly to forgive.
Hold on to forgiveness.

The REACH model of forgiveness is found in Worthington's *Forgiving and Reconciling: Bridges to Wholeness and Hope.*[2] It is based on his lifetime of experience with forgiveness and reconciliation as a Christian, clinical psychologist, and research professor. After writing his first book on forgiveness, *To Forgive Is Human*, Dr. Worthington's mother was murdered by a stranger in a senseless act of violence. He then challenged himself to use his own REACH method to forgive the murderer. His story appears in the film, *The Big Question: A Film About Forgiveness.*

Here is a brief overview of the REACH method of achieving forgiveness. You'll see the clear parallel with L-E-T G-O.

Recall the hurt: Think about the transgression against you as objectively as you can. The goal is to admit that you were wronged but without dwelling in the feelings around the hurt. From a place of greater objectivity we can move forward in healing.

Empathize: Forgiveness researchers focus on "walk a mile in the shoes" of the transgressor. By seeing from the other person's point of view, the hope is that the injured party can start to replace feelings of hurt, anger, revenge, and so on with some more positive feeling such as compassion.

Altruistic gift of forgiveness: Here, Dr. Worthington suggests you think of a time you hurt someone and were forgiven. Remembering the gift given to you may help you to give the gift to someone else.

Commit publicly to forgive: When you tell someone else about your gift of forgiveness it becomes more real and you are less likely later to doubt that you have forgiven.

Hold on to forgiveness: It's easy to think that memories of the hurt are the same as unforgiveness. They aren't. After you have forgiven the transgressor, memories of the hurt may return but now you can remind yourself that you are maintaining a new attitude toward the person and the event.

NOT EASY BUT NECESSARY

"Do not fear. Only believe" (Luke 8:50).

The process of rebuilding a broken relationship can seem daunting. You don't want to do it because it is hard, and you are afraid you may be met with anger. That is when you turn to God in prayer and trust that God will guide you along the way to forgiveness and letting go of a grudge. At every point of decision, you pray and ask God for direction. You check with friends or a spiritual advisor about the next right thing for you to do. You trust that God will provide not only direction but the strength to do what needs to be done.

If you are like me, you don't want to humble yourself and admit you are wrong. You don't want to confess your bad behavior and ask for forgiveness. Whenever I celebrate the sacrament of reconciliation with someone, I always begin with this passage:

> Since, then, we have a great high priest who has passed through the heavens, Jesus, the Son of God, let us hold fast to our confession. For we do not have a high priest who is unable to sympathize with our weaknesses, but we have one who in every respect has been tested as we are, yet without sin. Let us therefore approach the throne of grace with boldness, so that we may receive mercy and find grace to help in time of need. (Heb 4:14–16)

This passage reminds me to be a merciful confessor and offers hope to the ones making their confession that God already understands them and is offering them grace, that is, the strength to receive forgiveness and extend it to others. That strength is necessary because forgiveness and reconciliation aren't easy, but they are necessary.

NOTES

1. Thomas Merton, *New Seeds of Contemplation* (New York: New Directions, 1972), 72–76.
2. Everett L. Worthington, *Forgiving and Reconciling: Bridges to Wholeness and Hope*, (Downers Grove, IL: InterVarsity Press, 2003).

CHAPTER FOUR

WHY YOU DON'T WANT TO FORGIVE

Abraham Lincoln's capacity for forgiveness helped to heal the United States after the Civil War. His second inaugural address, delivered shortly before the end of the war, was a healing balm to the country: "with malice toward none and charity towards all." On the morning when he was shot, Lincoln was discussing with his advisors clemency for the Southern states. The opposite of forgiveness was shown by John Wilkes Booth, who said the reason he shot the president was because his side lost the war. Both men were seeking their own sense of justice. Both men sensed a gap in justice. President Lincoln wanted to heal the gapping wound that divided the United States. Booth simply wanted revenge.

JUSTICE AND FORGIVENESS

The biggest reason you don't want to forgive is because your sense of justice has been violated, and you think if you forgive that you are letting someone off the hook, letting the person get away with bad behavior and that you are condoning evil.

A sense of justice is deeply engrained in the human psyche. You want people to deal with you fairly and with respect. When they don't, you want to settle the score, you want to be made whole, you want justice. A good definition of "justice" is the golden rule: "Love your neighbor as you love yourself." Justice is treating other people as you want to be treated.

Justice is imperative for human beings because it is a part of God's nature. You are made in God's image and so justice is built into your nature as human beings. In the Bible, God is a God of both justice and mercy. There is a story in the Jewish Midrash (ancient commentary on the Hebrew Scriptures) that God created the world twice. First, God created a perfectly just universe. But, because human beings could not practice perfect justice, the universe immediately self-destructed. God created the universe again, and this time it was based on both God's justice and mercy. This is the universe we live in.

In both the Old and New Testaments of the Bible, people are called to practice the virtue of justice. "You shall not be partial to the poor or defer to the great: with justice you shall judge your neighbor" (Lev 19:15). "Masters, treat your slaves justly and fairly, for you know that you also have a Master in heaven" (Col 4:1). Throughout the Bible, the one thing that makes God angry is injustice.

Forgiveness that skips over justice is not real forgiveness; it is cheap forgiveness, that is, it is really just submission to the transgressor. Bypassing justice turns forgiveness into a way of the weak rather than the way of the strong. Justice demands that you confront a wrong when you meet it.

It helps to realize there are two different kinds of justice. There is *retributive justice*, the sort of justice our penal system is based on, that punishes people for doing something wrong. It is a way to extract the debt someone owes. It is eye-for-an-eye justice. God taught about retributive justice in the Bible:

Anyone who kills a human being shall be put to death. Anyone who kills an animal shall make restitution for it, life for life. Anyone who maims another shall suffer the same injury in return: fracture for fracture, eye for eye, tooth for tooth; the injury inflicted is the injury to be suffered. One who kills an animal shall make restitution for it; but one who kills a human being shall be put to death. (Lev 24:17–21)

This teaching limits the amount of restitution a victim is allowed. If someone poked out your eye, you could poke out their eye, but you couldn't kill them. The law was about limiting revenge. A transgressor could be punished by doing to him what he had done to the victim, but that was it. The victim could not exact a greater punishment. In our legal system we would say that the victim could get restitution but not damages. Limiting vengeance was a way to break the cycle of escalating retribution and violence that happens in any kind of a feud or war.

The other sort of justice is *restorative justice*. Restorative justice wants to restore a broken relationship to its preoffense condition, in other words, restorative justice is about knitting back together the relationship that has been torn. This is the sort of justice that Sister Helen Prejean, CSJ, author of *Dead Man Walking* and an advocate to abolish the death penalty, talks about.

Forgiveness does not mean that you forgo restitution. Restitution may very well be part of restoring the relationship. A person may have to pay back what she owes to further the process of restoring the relationship, but if she can't or won't, you can still extend forgiveness. Remember, Jesus forgave from the cross even while the crowd still jeered him.

When you have been harmed, it is natural to want the

other person to be punished. You have suffered an injustice, and your mind craves that the situation be made right somehow. The problem is you may never see justice and even if you do, you may not regain a sense of emotional equilibrium. Seeing the execution of someone who murdered a loved one may bring a sense of completion to the process of justice, but it may not bring emotional healing. You may still feel hurt and resentful even if you see the perpetrator brought to justice. Forgiveness helps you move to a sense of peace and freedom in the here and now, leaving the past in the past.

Restorative justice is the sort of justice practiced by Archbishop Tutu when he led the Truth and Reconciliation Commission in South Africa. After the fall of apartheid, the country could have been torn apart by black-on-white civil war. Instead, people channeled the outrage over the injustice done to them into a system of restorative justice. The people who had tortured and murdered could seek to be restored to the community if they told the truth about their actions and asked forgiveness of the victims and their families. The perpetrators were subject to the criminal justice system, retributive justice, but they could also seek to find peace of mind and bring some peace to the victim and their families through restorative justice. In shorthand this means: the job of justice is to right wrongs. The job of forgiveness is to heal hurts. When justice is not done, you get angry. A primary reason you don't want to forgive is because you are angry.

THE COLORS OF ANGER

Anger is a normal human response; it's part of your defense system. Anger kicks in to protect you when you've been hurt and don't want to be hurt again. When you are angry, your body shifts into fight-or-flight mode. Your body readies itself to attack or run away. This sort of anger is how you are built; there is no moral judgment on it.

You can think of anger as a type of energy. Anger makes you feel powerful. It can go wild and cause all kinds of problems, or it can be domesticated and help you to solve problems. The difficult and great conversion of anger is to change it from raw energy that can destroy into a controlled energy that can be used for justice and healing. The spirituality of forgiveness enables you to change the raw energy of anger into a tool to solve problems.

You might think of anger as having different colors: red, purple, white, beige, blue, silver, and gold. Here's how the spectrum of anger might be striated:

> **Red anger** is the ordinary, day-to-day anger that flares up and dissipates quickly. Red anger occurs when someone cuts you off in traffic, or the person in front of you in the checkout lane unloads fifteen items onto the ten-items-or-less checkout counter at the grocery store, or your child for the third time that day dumps all his toys on the floor. You get angry, but you get over it.
>
> Your body senses a threat, your brain registers an injustice, but the threat goes away, the injustice is not that great, and you move on. It's the kind of anger you feel when someone bumps into you by accident but there is no real damage. When that bump results in a bruise, then you experience purple anger.
>
> **Purple anger** occurs when a resentment is the residual effect of the threat. The anger sticks around. You nurse the anger thinking about what happened to you; you stay sore. The anger doesn't go away. This is the kind of anger that starts to eat away at you

from the inside out. Mark Twain once said, "Anger is an acid that can do more harm to the vessel in which it is stored than to anything on which it is poured." People often say, "Resentment is anger past its freshness date" and "Resentment is the poison you drink and hope the other guy dies."

The word resentment comes from the Latin word *sentire* ("to feel") and the Latin prefix *re* ("again," as in "repeat"). So the word means "to feel again." You feel the hurt over and over again, and each time you feel the hurt, you are re-traumatizing yourself. You need to let go of the resentment and stop thinking about the hurt so that you can get past the pain. If the hurt done to you is great, or you do a good job fanning the flames of the resentment, the anger can turn white hot.

White anger is a combination of resentment and rage. This is the kind of anger that is called "wrath": white-hot anger bursts into crimes of passion. Wrath is the kind of anger that is listed among the seven deadly sins. This kind of anger is more than a bruise; it's a cancer.

Wrath is anger that has hardened into a malicious spirit. Wrath is the anger associated with vengeance and vigilantism. This is the kind of anger Jesus refers to in Matthew 5:21–26. Anger that turns into contempt and hardheartedness is what gets people into trouble. It's very hard to restore a relationship that has become poisoned by contempt; Jesus says it is better to not let it get there. Most everyone knows the danger of anger that is hot, out of control, and sharpened to a point. This is the kind of anger that leads to revenge.

Revenge is a normal response that has evolved in the brain to help humans seek justice and relieve themselves of pain. And revenge is fun. People like planning to get back at someone and seeing the other person get his comeuppance.

You see this most often in movies in which revenge is a common theme, especially action movies, thrillers, and slasher films. These films play to that part of your brain that enjoys revenge, that makes you feel powerful and able to even the score, and that feeds your desire to win. The trouble with revenge, however, is that it perpetuates a cycle of violence. Carried to its logical conclusion, revenge behavior means everybody dies.

Revenge is hitting back after the fight is over, trying to harm someone who has harmed you beyond the point of self-defense. When you are feeling safe and want to get back at the person, that is revenge.

The pertinent problem for you is that the desire for revenge can lead to obsessive thinking. Vengeful thoughts take on a life of their own. Like any addiction, vengeance robs you of freedom; instead of focusing on the things that lead to a fulfilled and joyful life, you become mired in a mud fight. And like any addiction, it has a short-term gain but long-term pain as you find yourself being led away from your true loves.

You may feel pumped up after you have gotten back at the person who hurt you, but after the false buzz of victory wears off, you get a hangover; you feel the short-term fun and long-term pain because you don't like yourself. If you have a conscience, you will realize that what you did wasn't good, and then you will think of yourself as not being a good person; you will get down on yourself. One of the aftereffects of revenge is that you have become mired in a mess of self-disgust.

Exercise to Deal with Revenge

Write about any feelings of revenge you have. Who do you want to get back at and why? How do you want to hurt the person(s)? What would be the aftermath for you and the other person if you acted on your revenge?

Many people don't get to the white-hot stage of revenge. They engage in cooler, duller forms of anger, like beige anger.

Beige anger is anger in hibernation. You don't recognize it as anger when you see it. It's a roly-poly kind of anger, it looks like eating junk food on the couch, it looks like having too much to drink. Beige anger is the whole-loaf-of-white-bread and half-a-bottle-of-booze anger; it is anything you can use to narcotize yourself so you don't notice that you are really angry. This is the passive-aggressive kind of anger; you figure out a way to get back at the other person but not get blamed for it. This kind of anger, when it gets choked, can turn blue.

Blue anger is what everybody has heard described as "the blues." When anger is suppressed, it turns into depression. Blue anger is anger that goes inward because you are afraid to direct it outward; if you show your anger, you are afraid of the consequences so you shut down; you hurt yourself rather than threaten someone else. As the old blues song says, "Sometimes we have to put our foot down to hold our head up." You have to change the anger from destructive to constructive.

THE ALCHEMY OF ANGER

How do you turn the energy of anger from being destructive to being constructive? Forgiveness is the lodestone, the one magic ingredient you can use to convert anger from something wild that can destroy into something good that can heal. Constructive anger is either silver or gold.

Silver anger is like a scalpel or hammer. When you forgive, you tame the raw energy of anger so that it can be used as a tool to solve problems, a tool like a hammer. In the words of the old civil rights tune, "If I had a hammer, I'd hammer out justice." *The Big Question* also had fine examples of silver anger in the actions of Martin Luther King and Archbishop Desmond Tutu.

Silver anger can be like a scalpel that can cut away a malignant growth. Properly directed anger can allow you to detach from a problem or a person that is hurting you. You don't have to smash the person to get away, but you can detach with love, which brings you to golden anger.

Golden anger is the anger of Jesus; it's the kind of anger that confronts evil but confronts with love rather than hate. Jesus knew the alchemy of anger. Jesus' anger is an energy that is ultimately healing. What gets Jesus angry is injustice, and he uses that anger to try to right the wrong. He was able to confront injustice and sin, name it, call it to conversion, and then either walk away from it ("shake the dust from your sandals") or change it, such as when he converted the tax collector Matthew into one of his disciples.

What makes this kind of anger golden is that, although Jesus had more reason than anyone else to be contemptuous of human beings, he both taught and lived "Love your enemies, pray for those who persecute you."

CHAPTER FIVE

THE BIG FORGIVES

Three "Big Forgives" mirror the three "Big Loves" found in the Golden Rule. Luke's Gospel reads:

> Just then a lawyer stood up to test Jesus. "Teacher," he said, "what must I do to inherit eternal life?" He said to him, "What is written in the law? What do you read there?" He answered, "You shall love the Lord your God with all your heart, and with all your soul, and with all your strength, and with all your mind; and your neighbor as yourself." And he said to him, "You have given the right answer; do this, and you will live." (Luke 10:25–28)

The Golden Rule covers all relationships. Who else is there to love besides God, your neighbor, and yourself? Because the ones you love are the ones most likely to hurt you, they— God, your neighbor, yourself—are also the ones who will inspire your anger. That means they are also the ones you will need to forgive in order to get past your anger. The Big Forgives are Forgive God, Forgive Your Neighbor, and Forgive Yourself.

The process you have entered is primarily about forgiving your neighbors who have hurt you, but looking at forgiving God and forgiving yourself is also valuable.

FORGIVING GOD

Forgiving God sounds like an odd concept. If you blame God for either doing something to you or allowing something to happen to you, then before you can grow in your relationship with God, you must seek some kind of reconciliation. Many people live many years with a profound or vague sense of alienation because they have stepped back from God due to some hurt the person suffered and blamed on God's action or inaction. In any situation you can feel that God should have been protecting you. Sometimes this hurt has happened in a church community.

On nearly every parish mission or retreat I preach, I meet at least one person who is there because someone in their church has hurt them. Some examples of people who felt hurt by their church include:

- A woman struggling with her anger at the bishop who overlooked the harm caused by a priest who molested her son. In this case she wanted to take action to call the bishop to accountability, but she wanted to do it with love in her heart and not hate.
- A mother wanting to forgive a religious leader who tried to recruit her son into a particularly cult-like group.
- A young woman angry at her church for overlooking mistakes her pastor had made; members of her congregation wanted her to forgive, but she felt that the sort of forgiveness they wanted her to show was cheap because it didn't acknowledge the real harm her pastor had done.
- An older woman who didn't understand why she was excluded from a church group. She didn't

want to be eaten up by the bitterness she felt toward the group.

All these people are good people who have tried to do good things, and yet, they feel that the one group that should reward and protect them has failed them. They can't help but ask "Why?" "Where is God in this situation?" "Shouldn't God take better care of me?"

Whenever you hear a story of some terrible thing happening to a good person, it is natural to ask, "Why didn't God protect that person?" This opens up the profound question, "If God is good, why does God allow evil to happen?"

This is the question Job asks. This is the great question theologians and philosophers have struggled with from the beginning of monotheism. The question of why there is evil in the world is not a problem to be solved because no one can ever fully comprehend the nature of evil and why it exists. Fundamentally, it's a mystery each person lives with. But there are approaches that help a person to do so.

One approach to the mystery of evil is to know that it is a consequence of free will. God created you to be like God, free to make choices and be creative. You can choose for good and you can choose for bad. The story of Adam and Eve offers the paradigm of making a selfish choice, a choice not in God's will. The story tells that by their choice evil entered the world. There is a way to see evil in the world as the myriad consequences of all the bad choices people have made since the beginning of time.

How do you live with the mystery of evil in the world? The simple approach is to know that God is love and created you to love. God has given you the freedom to love or not. When you choose not to love, all manner of evil springs forth. God does not take back your freedom in order to end evil; rather, God works with you to use your freedom to promote good. When you forgive, you are making a loving choice to renounce evil and do good.

The answer to the question of evil with the longest tail is the devil. In this worldview, evil happens because the devil causes bad things to happen. Another worldview says that evil happens not because of the devil's will but because of random chance; life is a dice game and sometimes you win and sometimes you lose. No matter what answer you come to about the question "Why do bad things happen to good people?" your reason may not be enough to stem the tide of anger you sometimes feel when you are outraged at life's circumstances. When you feel such outrage, it is okay to express your anger at God. Some people try to protect God from their anger, but God is big enough to handle your anger.

ANGER TOWARD GOD

When something bad happens to you, you want to blame someone or something. If there is no person to blame, you may blame God. "God, why did you do this to me?" Rather than seeing anger at God as a sin, you can see it as an invitation to deeper intimacy with God. If you express your anger, it may help you delve deeper into your relationship with God. If you don't express your anger, the alternative may be to turn away from God and break off your relationship.

Anger in itself is not a sin. The sin is when you give into the anger and lash out and do some harm. The sin is holding onto the anger and letting it fester into resentment and contempt. Psalm 4:4 tells us "When you are disturbed, do not sin." Holding onto the anger is a sin. In Matthew's Gospel, Jesus says, "But I say to you that if you are angry with a brother or sister, you will be liable to judgment; and if you insult a brother or sister, you will be liable to the council; and if you say, 'You fool,' you will be liable to the hell of fire" (5:22). The Hebrew word Jesus uses for "fool" connotes a scoundrel, someone who is both stupid and morally corrupt. It is an expression of contempt, the kind of contempt that breaks off all relationship. This is what God does not want you to do: to use your anger to hold people in contempt. When a relationship reaches the stage of contempt, then any sort of Christian relationship is ended.

Jesus became angry at the religious leaders of his time. They opposed his message of good news and healing. He got angry at them because they were religious leaders who should have understood and supported his message, but instead they tried to turn him into an outcast. The most famous example of this is when Jesus drove the money changers out of the temple. He was angry that the place of worship had been desecrated by the commercial practices surrounding the temple activities (John 2:15–16). Jesus' anger was inspired by his love of God. His anger is a sign of his intimacy with God. Jesus also got angry with St. Peter, calling him Satan (Matt 16:22–23). Jesus was close to people, close enough that he could risk getting angry and he knew Peter would stick around, and, in fact, become the leader of the disciples.

Christ's intimacy with God is shown in his cry from the cross: "My God, my God, why have you forsaken me?" (Matt 27:46). This is an expression of anguish, but under the anguish you can read that Christ was angry at God for abandoning him. From the cross Jesus showed that a relationship with God includes being angry. If Jesus in the midst of his suffering can be angry with God, so can you.

Another example of anger at God can be found in the prophet Jeremiah 20:7, 8b, 9:

> O Lord, you have enticed me, and I was enticed;
> you have overpowered me, and you have pre-
> vailed. I have become a laughingstock all day
> long....The word of the Lord has become for me a
> reproach and derision all day long. If I say, "I will
> not mention him, or speak any more in his name,"
> then within me there is something like a burning
> fire shut up in my bones...." (Jer 20:7–13)

Jeremiah was angry with God but didn't end his relationship with God. His relationship was too much a part of him for him to walk away from God. He got angry but didn't let the anger lead him into sin, that is, to breaking off his relationship with God.

When you are angry with God, the thing to do is express your anger to God but not let the anger turn you away from God. Channel the anger into prayer and then listen in your heart for some response. Perhaps what you will meet is God's compassion. You may never understand why the evil happened, but you may meet the face of God who has suffered with you.

FEELING SYMPATHY FOR GOD

Christians believe that God understands how you feel because his own son, Jesus Christ, suffered from evil—his unjust and painful death on the cross. Evil happens and sometimes it happens to good people who didn't do anything to deserve it. As a Christian, you must remember that God entered into evil, wept with us, experienced evil deeply on the cross, and overcame it. Now, it is your turn to overcome evil and choose to forgive. Perhaps one of the Big Forgives is to forgive God. If you are angry at God, then you need to forgive God so that you can move on with your spiritual life.

How do you forgive God? Doesn't it seem presumptuous to think about offering God forgiveness? When I was a young child, I thought my dad was the best and could do no wrong. He was always cool and collected. One day while on vacation, he promised to take me to an arcade. I was eager to go, and he was taking his time. He was in vacation mode and I was in high gear. I turned into a pest and yammered at him, telling him to hurry up. In reaction to my hectoring, he hurried his shaving and cut his face more than once. When he came out of the bathroom with flecks of tissue stopping the cuts on his face, I felt awful. I had caused him to rush, and he had hurt himself. Suddenly my impression of him as perfect and unflappable was shattered. He could be frazzled too. I felt ashamed for nagging him and felt sorry that he had hurt himself. It was the first time I felt sympathy for my father.

Can you feel sympathy for God? God gave us creation and life. God wants you to co-create good with good lives and a good world. You can build paradise or hell. If you were God, how would you feel when you see your children striving to co-create paradise? If you were God, how would you feel when he sees the hell people have created over the centuries and continue to create?

Feeling sympathy for God may help to forgive God. We understand that God has given us what we need to create a wonderful world. God wants good for us, but so often we human beings choose evil, which causes great harm to God's creation. We have betrayed God. When we grasp this, then perhaps we can have sympathy for God.

FORGIVING YOURSELF

To become a forgiving person and to live at peace with yourself you have to be able to love and forgive yourself. Forgiving yourself is an inside job, but those who believe in God have an inestimable resource outside of themselves to call on. It is easier to forgive yourself when you know that God loves you and wants you to live at peace.

God loves you essentially, that is, God loves the essence of you. God loves that which makes up your very being. Surely there are things you do that God does not love, and there are things you do that disappoint and grieve God. There are consequences for your behavior that feel like punishment, but you are more than the sum total of your actions. At your heart, at your essence, at the level of what makes you human along with everyone else is the fact that God loves you.

God loves his children the way a parent loves a growing child. Children make mistakes, but they can be guided from their mistakes to more life-giving behavior. God wants the absolute best for you. God's love is constant. When you can accept this grace, then you are able to love yourself, and you are able to extend this same grace to others.

You must be able to forgive yourself and others because you and everyone else are subject to the human condition of original sin. You get your own little piece of original sin when you join the human race.

MY PIECE OF ORIGINAL SIN

My own little piece of original sin, which really isn't so little, is a big share of gluttony. I grew up eating more than I needed, and so at an early age broke out in fat. Growing up overweight was no fun, nor was shopping for "husky" pants, not being included in sports, suffering embarrassment in gym class, and looking more awkward than the average kid in puberty. The hurt didn't abate when I hit adulthood; it was just a wider me in a wider arena.

I realized that I didn't have a normal relationship with food. Normal people get hungry, they eat and get full, and they stop eating. I ate when I wasn't hungry. I continued to eat when I was full. I was eating not because I was physically hungry but because I was eating to comfort myself when I felt anxious. Eating has long been my reaction to stress; I am a stress eater.

The result of stress eating is being overweight and realizing that fat people don't get much approval in society. Thin is in. For me, this led to growing up with a sense of shame; I didn't like myself. Also, I didn't like other people who were overweight. The shadow side of myself that I saw in them set me up to judge them as harshly as I judged myself.

When I realized that my reaction to others was rooted in my own lack of self-worth, then I could really start to listen to others. As I let in their stories, let in their pain, I could feel compassion for them. But before that could happen, I had to develop a sense of compassion for myself.

Understanding why I was eating more than my body needed didn't give me the power to stop. In my experience, the truth did not set me free; the truth was a step to freedom. I also needed to feel loved by God in a very practical way; I needed to know that God could help me to stop overeating.

One day when I was praying, I slipped into something between a coma and a daydream. Suddenly I was standing at the foot of the cross. Next to me was a Roman soldier with a spear in his hand. He stuck a sponge on the end of the spear and put the sponge in a wooden bucket of what I knew was drugged wine. The soldier held the sponge up to Jesus' mouth. Jesus turned his face away from the wine, looked over the shoulder of the soldier, straight at me with eyes that riveted me to the spot and said, "If I can say no to my drug, you can so no to yours."

This was a revelation. This was my "Paul on the road to Damascus" experience. If Jesus could go through the crucifixion (surely a stress if ever there was one) and reach out to me to offer me strength, then I knew that I could put up with my lesser sufferings without eating compulsively.

Jesus' love from the cross allowed me to start to love myself and forgive myself for the years of overeating and being overweight and all that the weight had wrought in my life. In loving myself, I developed a deeper sense of compassion for other people who had the same struggle.

I also found that being with other people dealing with the same problem and sharing in their struggles and victories provides another avenue through which God's strength and hope can operate as they help me and I help them.

EMPATHY FOR YOURSELF

Just as you must develop empathy for a transgressor in order to forgive him or her, so you need to develop empathy for yourself to forgive yourself. You have to see the truth of your life and how you have been hurt, how you have hurt yourself and how you must be willing to let go of self-blame and move toward self-acceptance.

Earlier I mentioned one mind trick: the exquisite ability to rationalize bad behavior. The opposite mind trick is to be your own worst enemy. Before realizing the truth behind my overeating and before accepting God's love and help in my life, I alternated between two behaviors: self-justification and self-loathing. I was either making excuses for myself or I was my harshest critic.

You might ask yourself: Do I forgive my friends more easily than I forgive myself? If I treated my friends the way I treat myself, would I have any friends?

FORGIVE YOURSELF

If you find yourself holding a grudge against yourself, that is, you can't forgive yourself for something, ask yourself if what you feel is guilt or shame. Author John Bradshaw distinguishes between the two: guilt = I made a mistake; shame = I am a mistake.

Ask yourself what you are feeling: do you feel guilt for a mistake you made, or do you feel shame for who you are? The first may require you to make some restitution for the mistake so that you can take responsibility for your actions, and then, with a clean slate, move forward in your life. The second, a sense of shame, needs to be replaced with a positive sense of self. As the old saying goes, "God doesn't make junk." You may want to apologize to yourself for accepting the shame that someone else placed on you and then place that shame in God's hands and ask God to remove it.

Sometimes you haven't really done anything wrong, but you may have to forgive yourself anyway. Jane was someone who needed to forgive herself. A successful artist and businesswoman, she described herself as someone who "escaped from a white-trash family." When she was a young teenager, she was sexually abused, raped really, by a family member. For years, she lived with a deep sense of shame that colored her outlook on life and on herself. She felt dirty and bad. She felt that somehow she was responsible for what happened to her. Finally, after years of therapy and a religious conversion, she was able to forgive herself, realize that she wasn't to blame, and develop a healthy sense of herself and her sexuality. She was able to forgive the man who raped her, but only after she made the decision never to see him or talk to him again. She had to completely detach from him before she could forgive him and let go of the burden that horrible incident had attached to her life.

Jane said the hardest thing she had to do was to forgive herself. First of all, she had to let go of taking any responsibility for somehow causing the rape. Then, she had to let go of the guilt she carried for blaming herself for all those years that she held herself back from living a full life. She said she felt like the forgiveness rewired her to be able to have a more fulfilled life.

Once, a woman came to me and said she had to forgive herself because she blamed herself for having cancer. She was caught up with persistent thoughts that asked her what she did to get the cancer. Despite the fact that she had a high risk of breast cancer because of her family history, she kept thinking it was her fault because of something she had done: bad diet, lack of exercise. In fact, she lived a healthy lifestyle, but she kept looking for what she did wrong.

You do need to forgive yourself for being human, especially when you try and play God. You forget you are just a boy or girl trying to figure out how to play in the sandbox together. You need to feel some empathy for yourself, realize you are fallible. Society says we must be self-reliant and so we expect perfection of ourselves. "Be perfect as your heavenly father is perfect." You can't do that on your own, you can only grow into the image of God by God's grace.

SUBSTITUTE POSITIVE FOR NEGATIVE THOUGHTS

When you are feeling down on yourself, when you are in the grips of self-pity, one thing that works is to keep substituting positive for negative thoughts. Once when I was going through a rough patch on the road of life, a road rutted with lots of self-doubt and self-pity, I decided that whenever I caught myself thinking about how badly things were going for me, I would substitute a positive thought for that negative thought. Sometimes I would focus on something that was right in front of me for which I was grateful—a beautiful scene, a dear friend, an enjoyable meal, a clean room. Thinking positively helped to keep me in a lighter mood.

Other such practices include:

Focus on your strengths. Make a list of what you are good at doing and what virtues others see in you. Name the talents and gifts you have that benefit others. Are you quick to help? Are you a good listener? Do you create beauty that delights others? Are you helpful? Are you kind? Do you offer good counsel?

Do good for others. If you are feeling pinned down by the critic in your own head, escape from your scolding and do something good for someone else.

Cultivate compassion. Recognize in others the same joys and hurts that you yourself experience. Reach out to others with a message of care. Call someone you haven't talked to in awhile and ask the person how he or she is doing.

Hold love in your heart. Think of someone who loves you and hold the thought of that person in your heart. Ask yourself, "Why does she love me?" **Ask what you've learned.** The value gleaned from your mistakes is what you learn from them. If you can fashion a lesson for yourself, you have gained a coin of wisdom that you can pass along to someone else, or use to your advantage in the future.

BE GRATEFUL FOR SMALL GRACES

Forgiving yourself may involve breakthroughs, like my experience of Jesus on the cross, but more likely, self-forgiveness happens gradually.

Perhaps you've heard it said, "If you want to build self-esteem, do estimable things." It's good to remember all the estimable things you have done. One way to think about this is to picture a box of photos in your head that show the good times and bad times in your past, times when you were proud of who you are and what you did, and photos of times you were ashamed of how you behaved. In forgiving yourself, it's a wise idea to put the photos of the self you love in a mental slide show and play that slide show over and over. The rest of the photos, the ones that aren't as flattering, you will want to leave in the box.

In forgiving yourself, you need to be grateful for small graces. If you don't like yourself because of your quick temper and just once you catch yourself taking a deep breath and not yelling when you lose your temper, be grateful for that small grace of change. Faults don't disappear all at once; you make progress by inches.

The Big Forgives happen through Big Love. You suspend blame, you stop blaming God for something that happened to you, you stop blaming yourself for some mistake you made or flaw you have, you suspend blame of some perpetrator for harm caused, even if the person deserves blame. In place of that blame, you substitute empathy. You feel some sympathy for yourself and the hurt you've endured, for God whose creation has been betrayed, for the other person who is so flawed that he or she would perpetrate a hurt. That wedge of sympathy you feel can begin to open the door to letting go of old anger and pain. Once you can let go, you can let in healing and new growth.

CHAPTER SIX

LOOK DEEPLY AT WHAT WENT WRONG

Forgiveness begins with honesty. You need to be aware of the reality of your own life. First, you understand deeply that you are a good creation of a God who wants the best for you. Then you admit that you are a creature with a wavering will and limitations, and you understand yourself as imperfect. You suffer from the human condition of being born as a good being into a fallen world and sharing a fallen human nature. Your fallen nature can be seen in the mind tricks you play. You have an exquisite capacity for self-deception. You may not be athletic, but you can water ski on the river of denial.

TELL YOUR STORY

A good place to start your deep and long look at what went wrong is to tell the story to someone who is supportive and objective and can help you see the situation through another pair of eyes. Your purpose in telling the story is not to elicit sympathy or to blame the person who hurt you or to justify your actions but to get at the truth. This is helpful when the conflict is with someone you know and with whom you will continue to interact, such as a coworker, family member, or friend.

If the perpetrator is a stranger to you, perhaps a criminal who only came into your life to perpetrate the crime or a drunk driver who injured you, then looking deeply at your part of the story is not necessary. In most situations between two people, however, there are two sides to the story. You want to look at both sides.

You can't do this work of forgiveness alone. You need a community to heal. You must be willing to ask others to help you. It could be a religious professional, a professional counselor, or a professional barber. It could be a closed-mouth friend or a discrete hairdresser. The point is it's good to have another person who is detached from the incident who will review it with you, to see: What happened? What really happened? What did the other person do? What was your part?

You might find it helpful to write out the story of what happened as if you were a disinterested news reporter. Tell the story from a third-person point of view. Telling the story to an objective person or writing it out like a news story will help you gain some detachment from the hurtful incident and give you the emotional space to start to move forward in the work of forgiveness.

LOOK DEEPLY AT YOUR INNER LIFE

A next level of looking deeply is to examine and name your feelings around the transgression as well as toward the person who hurt you. This will help you to gain insight and make progress in the healing process. Perhaps you have heard it said, "The only way out is through." You need to name the feelings, discover what they are, before you can move beyond them. Emotions arise as part of your biological makeup to give you information about how to respond in the world.

Some people have a better emotional vocabulary than

others, but all of us on a physical level understand the Big Four: Mad, Glad, Sad, and Afraid. These four emotions can be traced in your body; there are physiological reactions. You can see these feelings on someone's face. When you are angry, your blood pressure rises. When you are afraid, your palms sweat. When you are glad, you smile. When you are sad, you frown and your stomach may hurt.

Anger, say some, is fear with an attitude. Fear and anger are two sides of the same coin. The flight or fight (fear/anger) response helps you to protect yourself: you defend or flee depending on the size of the threat. But no matter what response you choose, physiologically your body is ready for either. Some common feelings behind unforgiveness include:

Disappointment. "I didn't get what I wanted."
Rejection/self-doubt. "He/she pushed me away. What's the flaw in me?"
Abandonment. "I was left alone and insecure."
Loss. "I lost trust. I lost someone important to me."
Humiliation. "I was mocked. I didn't deserve to be ridiculed."
Betrayal. "I trusted them, and they destroyed my confidence."
Deception. "They lied to me."
Abuse. "They hurt me physically or emotionally. I'm damaged."
Insecurity. "I have lost a sense of safety."

Sometimes it's enough to name the feeling to help move it along and up and out of your psyche. A woman whose husband died unexpectedly of a heart attack in his fifties told me that she loved him very much and missed him terribly. She was locked in grief, but there was some other nagging feeling infecting that grief. A friend suggested that she write down ten things she wanted to forgive her husband for doing to her. She did and was surprised to find how easily the list emerged.

After his death, she had started to canonize her husband as a saint, but in fact, he was a flawed human. At first she didn't realize that she was carrying some anger toward him for things he had done during their marriage. The greatest thing she had to forgive was his abrupt departure from her life. It wasn't his fault, but still she displaced anger onto him.

After she made the list of ten things to forgive, she called her friend and read her the list. As a consequence of naming what bothered her, she found some wiggle room in her grief, and her life felt unlocked. She could breathe again. She still misses her husband, but she has now been able to move on and find joy again with her friends and in her ordinary daily activities.

In this woman's case, there was a great deal of loss and mixed with it was some anger. For most people, any assault, insult, or hurt suffered involves both loss and anger. You go through a sense of diminishment. Something is missing; you have less than you had before. When you come to terms with this, you have to say goodbye, which is another way of saying let go.

One divorced woman moved out of her former home in a rush. She realized later that every time she drove close to that neighborhood she got a headache. A friend suggested that she go back to her house, where her ex-husband still lived, and say goodbye to it. She took her friend's advice and spent three hours going through the house, touching everything in it and saying goodbye. She sobbed all the way home, and uncontrollable guttural noises came from a place deep within her. She pulled over and called her friend, who said, "Congratulations, you are free."

One way to look deeply is to write about what you have lost because of the hurt you suffered and identify what would be a good way for you to say goodbye to these things. Designing a goodbye ritual will help you let go.

The two most common feelings associated with being hurt are sadness and anger. You have to first get in touch with these feelings, feel them, move through them, and then get beyond these feelings. Some people are conditioned to feel sadness but to suppress anger; for others, the opposite is true. Some have an easier time getting in touch with their anger and a harder time grieving a loss. In my work, I've found that often women identify more easily with the grief of a grievance, and men are more easily in touch with the anger of some outrageous act.

GRIEF GONE WILD

U.S. President John Adams said that grief sharpens understanding and softens the heart. This is true when grief is used well. When grief is avoided, it can rupture relationships. Some people avoid grief by turning its pain into something else. They get angry and start a fight. They get drunk, they tell bad jokes—all of which sounds like a traditional Irish wake!

When I'm helping people prepare for a funeral, I give one piece of advice: "Forgive everything." Grief makes people do crazy, unexpected, out-of-character things. Members of the family or friends may act out their grief in unusual ways, so it's best to give grieving people a lot of slack.

Funerals are times when old hurts can come back unchecked. Perhaps the deceased was the moderating force in some family feud, and now, with no referee, the old resentment erupts. Many people come to one of my retreats or parish missions because their families are broken after the death of a parent. Grief turned to anger may manifest as a fight over some detail of the funeral or a quarrel over the inheritance. No matter what the dispute, what happens spiritually is that hardheartedness pushes out compassion. Grief has wrapped itself in the armor of anger as protection against feeling of the loss of the loved one.

Forgiveness is the process of inviting compassion back into the situation. To get to compassion, first the protective coat of anger has to be recognized for what it is. It helps to name the anger for what it is—grief gone wild. Then the anger has to be dispersed by empathy, that is, some sort of heart-to-heart connection, some sort of understanding that the other person is a hurting human being, too. Once compassion is in place, then the gift of forgiveness can be offered.

Paul's letter to the Colossians says it well:

> But now you must get rid of all such things— anger, wrath, malice, slander, and abusive language from your mouth. Do not lie to one another, seeing that you have stripped off the old self with its practices and have clothed yourselves with the new self, which is being renewed in knowledge according to the image of its creator. (Col 3:8–10)

Getting rid of anger, wrath, and malice, and stopping the trash talk about the person who hurt you is much easier said then done. It will take the time that it takes. You have to rely on God and let God lead you. The fruit of forgiveness is that you no longer feel the pain of the loss, and the anger doesn't have a hold on you anymore.

You want to be careful not to forgive too quickly, a tendency with some Christians. "I'm a Christian so I forgive. I've forgiven, let's move on." Hold on. You rely on God's grace to forgive, and it is possible that God will work a small miracle in your life so that you do forgive immediately and completely. Grace, however, usually builds on nature. God works with and through who you are, through and with your natural inclinations, your emotions, your past, your talents, and your deficiencies in order to bring about healing from a hurt. You have to have the patience to work through the process; otherwise what you are offering to the other person is cheap forgiveness.

YOUR NEMESIS—THE ENEMY

Another character to look at deeply is a character called Nemesis. Nemesis was the ancient Greek goddess of punishment or vengeance. The word "nemesis" has come to mean anyone who is a bitter enemy that won't go away, the enemy who comes after you with a vengeance. While this is not everyone's experience, it is worthwhile to look at this character of Nemesis, even if you don't feel like your hurt was caused by an enemy.

Sometimes your nemesis whines and tries to make you feel sorry for him or her. Sometimes the nemesis bullies and tries to intimidate you. When any attack occurs, it is wise and healthy to erect an appropriate barrier to defend yourself. You need to build a wall—a low wall that allows easy access to each other or a higher wall that requires you climb a ladder to see over. However high the wall, you need to build it with charity rather than hostility. The way to do that is with prayer. The more your nemesis wheedles or attacks, the more you pray for the person, back away, and pile on bricks. High or low, it's good to keep the wall as long as you need it. You can stay behind it when you need to or open a door when you want.

Having said that, you need to remember that your nemesis is a person before he or she is an enemy. Human's natural tendency is to turn a nemesis into a demon. When you demonize the person who hurt you, you dehumanize them. You see this demonization all of the time, most visible in war.

Before every war the enemy is dehumanized; the enemy is called a devil to be exorcised or a cockroach to be stepped on. This is a dishonest way to set the situation. When you turn a person into a demon, you also tend to turn yourself into a victim. When you turn yourself into a victim, then you give up responsibility. You give up any of your responsibility for causing the problem, and you give up your responsibility for solving the problem. Everything becomes all the other's person's fault.

When you have a grievance against someone, your world shrinks. The grievance can become the center of your world. You are no longer *for* yourself; you are now *against* your nemesis. You wrap your anger around the scar tissue of a hurt, and the tissue festers, never heals. You think about it too much. Your thinking may be compulsive; you can't fall asleep without thinking about how you want to hurt the person who hurt you. You indulge in fantasies of revenge.

The person who hurt you, the perpetrator, easily becomes your nemesis. The person embodies everything you don't like in other people and in yourself. Rather than deposit all your hurt at the nemesis's door, you have to sort out how big, really, is the hurt caused. It's easy to demonize the perpetrator and expand the hurt they did. You may have to let some of the air out of your overblown hurt and shrink the demon so it's easier to deal with. One way to deflate the hurt is to write as objectively as possible about what the other person did to you.

Exercise to Describe Your Nemesis

Imagine that you have been asked to write a eulogy about the person who hurt you. The person's family will be present. You can't say the negative things you want to say. What are at least three good things you could truthfully say about the person who hurt you? Remember, your nemesis may very well be someone possessed by their own inner demons and act in truly reprehensible ways. Your nemesis may be just another scared little boy or girl trying to figure out how to play with all the other boys and girls. Tell the truth about the person, but remember to tell the truth with love.

YOUR NEMESIS—
THE DARK SIDE OF YOU

There is another nemesis besides your enemy. There is "my nemesis," that is, your dark side. This nemesis is your shadow side, the dark side of your human nature, the part you don't want to look at, the part that keeps getting you into trouble. Until you confront this other nemesis, she will keep getting you into trouble.

One thing that wraps me around an axle is when someone else acts in a way that exposes what I don't like about myself. If someone acts in a controlling or arrogant way, and I get unreasonably angry with the person, it's probably because I don't like the controlling and arrogant part of me. Some of the anger I have toward myself spills over to the other person. If I admit that I have these faults, name them, ask God to help me overcome them, and forgive myself for these imperfections, then I don't react as strongly to those faults in someone else.

Perhaps you've heard the old saying, "Whenever you point a finger at someone else, three more point back at you."

One day in prayer I saw that my nemesis was the shadow of me: all his faults were defects of my own character. I didn't want to kill my nemesis so much as to kill the dark side of me. At that point I could release my stranglehold and let him and me go free.

When you look deeply at the problem, you have to admit there are not only two sides to the story but two imperfect people involved. Just as you have to be careful not to say, "It's all that person's fault," you have to be careful not to say, "It's all my fault." Then you are avoiding the truth of the situation, going down the path of self-loathing, substituting guilt for anger. This will lead to depression. It's dishonest to say, "It's all my fault," when it is simply a way to avoid the hard work of forgiveness.

Exercise to Identify Hurt's Consequences

Answer these questions honestly: How have I hurt myself? How has it affected my life and the lives of those around me?

CHAPTER SEVEN

EMPATHY IS THE KEY

When it comes to one person forgiving another, experts agree that empathy is the key. Before any sort of forgiveness can occur, the victim needs to have some sort of human connection or insight into the perpetrator, that is, you see the other person as someone like yourself. You try to understand the situation of the other person and see the hurtful incident from the other person's point of view. You must, as the saying goes, walk a mile in the other person's shoes. You want to see if you can connect with some feeling from or fact about the other person's life that can give you insight into who she is or why he may have done what he did.

Empathy is a complex concept that covers a whole range of responses. Some ways you may say "empathy" include:

"I think I understand."
"Oh, that poor thing."
"Oh, that poor man/woman."
"I feel for her."
"I want to help him."
"I love her."

To better understand empathy, you will want to look deeper at these very human reactions to another human being.

DEVELOPING EMPATHY

"I think I understand" is a way of expressing the most basic kind of empathy, an intellectual grasp of the other person's basic humanity and personality. On the level of understanding, your intellect is involved more than your emotions. This is the sort of empathy you might have for a sociopath, someone who has no conscience or is so selfish or emotionally disconnected that he truly doesn't care about other people's feelings.

"Oh, that poor thing" is the beginning of emotional identification, but you are identifying with the other as less than a full human being. You are identifying with a "thing" instead of a person. You have some feeling for the other person but still want to keep a distance from the person by objectifying the person. It's the kind of empathy you might have for a person living on the street. You have an emotional reaction but it is not so much toward the individual as it is sadness that a human being would be in that situation. You don't really want to engage the other person, but rather you "feel sorry" at a distance. You might call this pity.

"Oh, that poor man/woman" is what you say when you have moved from pity to sympathy. Being sympathetic means you are emotionally engaged with the other person, and you recognize the person's humanity. You don't really want to engage with the person, but you start to identify with her situation, and you start to put yourself in her place. If it's a street person, you might drop a coin in his cup.

"I feel for them." Once, when in the kitchen of a friend whose beloved family dog of sixteen years, Dobbie, had recently died, I spotted on the refrigerator this note scrawled in crayon by the little girl who lived next door:

Dear Jane, I'm sorry about Dobbie. Emily

In this case "I'm sorry" means I feel for you. The little girl simply says, "I share your grief." Emily knew Dobbie, and she too felt grief at the loss of this friendly playmate in her life. This feeling is called *compassion*. You put yourself in the other person's skin, and you literally "suffer with them" as the Latin roots of this word say (*passio* = "to suffer"; *com* = "with").

"I want to help." This is an expression of *love*, the fraternal love that in Greek is expressed in the word *agape*. This is the kind of love you as a Christian are called to extend to others. You put yourself in the other person's place and, as the Golden Rule advises, "love your neighbor as you love yourself."

"I love her." Romantic love, *eros*, is another sort of love. Romantic love is the pretty screensaver that gets you into the more complex program of *agape* love. Once you get past the initial infatuation of romantic love, then you really have to roll up your sleeves and do the real work of love. To feel what another is feeling, to want the best for that person, and to be willing to act in a way that shows that you carry the person's best interests in your heart is the real work of love.

Developing empathy is being able to see yourself as doing something similar to what was done to you, to stand on the common ground of your shared humanity. Once, a priest said to me during the sacrament of reconciliation, "There is nothing that you've done or thought that I haven't done or thought about. You can tell me anything." That was the permission I needed to be honest and to know that I'd be met with empathy and not condemnation.

For believers, prayer can be a gateway to empathy when you are having a hard time feeling any. You can pray for the gift of empathy. Ultimately, you find the common ground of your humanity with another that comes from the same Creator. You can pray to God to help you feel for the other person. Ask God to help you have some understanding and compassion for the other person. In order to accomplish the hard work of forgiveness, you need God's help.

The first letter of Peter provides inspiration for forgiving:

> Finally, all of you, have unity of spirit, sympathy, love for one another, a tender heart, and a humble mind. Do not repay evil for evil or abuse for abuse; but, on the contrary, repay with a blessing. It is for this that you were called—that you might inherit a blessing. (1 Pet 3:8–9)

PRAY FOR THE OTHER PERSON

If empathy for the other is key to forgiving, then a key to empathy is praying for the other person. Praying for the other person is your best tool in the work of forgiveness. There is a dual benefit in praying for the other person: First, prayer for the other is a blessing for *that person*. You are asking God's blessing on the person. You ask God to be present to the person, you extend your love to the person magnified through the all-powerful love of God.

The second benefit of praying for the person is that it is a blessing for *you*. When you hold another person in prayer, you will find that it becomes more difficult to hold hard feelings for him or her. When you pray for the other person, your heart softens and you open yourself to empathy for the person.

From personal experience, I have found that there is a relationship between the size of the hurt and how long I have to pray for the other person before my heart starts to soften toward the person and I start *feeling* forgiveness for him or her. With little hurts I can pray for the person in my night prayer and feel better about the person in the morning. With medium-size hurts, it takes one to three weeks of praying for the other person to experience forgiveness. With ongoing hurts, I must pray for the person every day, sometimes several times a day.

Getting to this sort of pure prayer takes awhile when you are holding a grudge. You will go through stages of praying for the other person:

> Admit you don't want to do it.
> Pray anyway through gritted teeth.
> Pray the person gets what he or she deserves.
> Pray that God will grant the person what you want for yourself.
> Pray that God will give the person what he or she wants to be happy.
> Pray that God will bless the person, as God wants to bless him or her.

Admit you don't want to do it. In any sort of prayer, honesty is the avenue through which you seek God. God is the ultimate truth and so to approach ultimate truth, you have to be honest about your truth and bring what is true to God. If you are feeling hatred, then admit that is how you feel and bring your hate into your prayer. Admit to God what God already knows: that you don't want to pray for the person who hurt you. Prayer is a gift, and you may not feel like giving the person a gift. You can, however, start the prayer from a stance of pity for the person who hurt you.

A story from Viktor Emil Frankl, the Austrian psychiatrist who survived three years in three different Nazi concentration camps, illustrates the value of praying for the person who hurt you. After his release from the camp, Frankl wrote *Man's Search for Meaning* and founded the school of psychotherapy known as existential therapy which was based on his experiences in the camps. He believed that when the physical life became intolerable, the spiritual life allowed someone to go on.

One day when Frankl was praying, a fellow prisoner asked him how he could pray, how he could believe in a God when there was such suffering all around him. Frankl pointed to an SS guard and said, "You see that man. I pray to God in gratitude that I was made me and not him." Viktor Frankl's prayer saved him from despair.

Pray anyway through gritted teeth. A teacher who had taught at the same inner-city school for years was much respected and had received "teacher of the year" at her school more than once. A new principal came to the school and for some reason disliked this teacher and wanted her fired. The situation had racial overtones since the teacher was African American and the new principal was white. The teacher, a Christian, knew she was to "love your enemies, pray for your persecutors." She felt unjustly persecuted, so every day as she walked into the school, she prayed for her principal, "God bless that son of a bitch."

Here is a prayer you can say through gritted teeth:

God, [fill in the blank with the person's name] is a
    twisted soul.
Save me from being angry.
Help me to see how I can be helpful, not hurtful.
May your will be done. Bless us both. Amen.

Pray the person gets what he or she deserves. This should be an easy prayer since it feels more like a curse than a blessing. If what you feel is a desire for revenge, then perhaps the most honest prayer is to ask God to exact vengeance for you. There is ancient precedent of asking God to act with justice on behalf of the innocent (see the next section on the Cursing Psalms). Recognize that you are letting God—not you—decide what the person deserves and that God may be more lenient in judgment than you. In all honesty, this may be the best you can do. Perhaps it will serve as a gateway to help you get to a more selfless prayer.

> Never avenge yourselves, but leave room for the wrath of God; for it is written, "Vengeance is mine, I will repay, says the Lord." No, "if your enemies are hungry, feed them; if they are thirsty, give them something to drink; for by doing this you will heap burning coals on their heads." Do not be overcome by evil, but overcome evil with good. (Rom 12:19–21)

Pray that God will grant the person what you want for yourself. As you can see, each stage of prayer is based less in anger and more in altruism. As you go through the stages, you are letting go of revenge and putting the relationship more and more in God's hands. You are softening your hard heart toward the other person. Perhaps you will even be able to pray that God will give the person what you want for yourself.

Pray that God will give the person what he or she wants to be happy. If one reason for praying for the other person is to help you develop empathy, then praying for his or her happiness is concrete evidence that you see the person as another of God's creations. This prayer is not a self-centered prayer where you are trying to control the situation through prayer, but rather an unselfish prayer that acknowledges the person as another human being who wants the same thing that you want.

Pray God will bless the person, as God wants to bless him or her. When you pray that God blesses the person as God wants to bless him or her, then you have achieved genuine prayer. Everything else prior to this is just telling God what to do. Finally, in this stage, you let go of the situation between you and the other person and put it in God's hands. When you ask God to bless as God wants to bless, then you are letting God be God. You are doing the "your will be done" part of the Our Father.

PRAYING AGAINST YOUR ENEMY

Praying for your enemy is a key way to develop empathy and free yourself from bondage to the past hurt. It is a way to carry out Jesus' command to "love your enemies, pray for those who persecute you." That's true, but, perhaps, you may first need to pray *against* your enemies before you can pray *for* your enemies.

Your ancestors in faith who wrote the Hebrew Scriptures were adept at praying against their enemies.

Psalms of Lament

There are one hundred and fifty psalms in the Book of Psalms, as many as sixty-seven can be classified as a psalms of lament. A psalm of lament is a prayer addressed to God which registers a complaint with God, asks God do something about the complaint, and ends with an expression of trust in God's power.

The lament is about some injustice done to the person praying the psalm. Some laments are corporate, that is, they are a complaint about God's actions toward or inaction on behalf of God's people. Sometimes the laments are personal, about an injustice or sadness that the individual is experiencing. In every case, the person praying appeals to God to correct the injustice.

Sometimes victims of an offense start to believe that they deserve the harm done to them. They internalize the hate the perpetrator shows them and start to hate themselves. What can help them to reclaim a sense of their self-worth is a psalm of lament. In praying a psalm of lament, you acknowledge your hurt, your loss, the injustice done to you. You release the power of your anger toward the perpetrator using the language of violence. You don't do the violence; you ask God to exact the vengeance on your enemy. By giving God the job of vengeance, you release yourself from having to do violence. This gives you a way to articulate the injustice and narrow the gap between what is and what should be.

Once you turn your vengeance over to God, leave it there. From now on, when you think of the person who hurt you, you can let go of revenge. You can now take the path that leads to a higher human development. Instead of being a creature of curses, you can be a creature of blessing. You are now free to say, "God bless my nemesis." You can say of all people, "God bless," and hope for them what is truly best for them. You can now be open to God's blessings in your own life and what is truly good for you.

Curse Your Enemy

The laments that follow are known as imprecatory psalms, that is, psalms that invoke a curse on an enemy. These psalms allow the one praying them to make a case before God and appeal to God's justice and abhorrence of evil.

You can read the psalms of lament with their cursing verses for yourself (see Ps 35, 55, 56, 57, 58, 69, 83, 88, 109, 137, 139, and 140).

Let's read through Psalm 140 and then look at what it says.

Deliver me, O LORD, from evildoers;
    protect me from those who are violent,
who plan evil things in their minds
    and stir up wars continually.
They make their tongue sharp as a snake's,
    and under their lips is the venom of vipers. Selah
Guard me, O LORD, from the hands of the wicked;
    protect me from the violent who have planned my
        downfall.
The arrogant have hidden a trap for me,
    and with cords they have spread a net,
    along the road they have set snares for me. Selah

I say to the LORD, "You are my God;
    give ear, O LORD, to the voice of my supplications."
O LORD, my Lord, my strong deliverer,
    you have covered my head in the day of battle.
Do not grant, O LORD, the desires of the wicked;
    do not further their evil plot. Selah

Those who surround me lift up their heads;
    let the mischief of their lips overwhelm them!
Let burning coals fall on them!
    Let them be flung into pits, no more to rise!
Do not let the slanderer be established in the land;
    let evil speedily hunt down the violent!

I know that the LORD maintains the cause of the needy,
    and executes justice for the poor.
Surely the righteous shall give thanks to your name;
    the upright shall live in your presence.

You can see the structure of this psalm:

> Deliver me, O Lord, from evildoers;
>> protect me from those who are violent,
> who plan evil things in their minds
>> and stir up wars continually.

The psalmist is asking for God's protection from violent and evil people. I can honestly pray that myself.

> They make their tongue sharp as a snake's,
>> and under their lips is the venom of vipers.
> Guard me, O Lord, from the hands of the wicked;
>> protect me from the violent who have planned my
>>> downfall.
> The arrogant have hidden a trap for me,
>> and with cords they have spread a net,
>> along the road they have set snares for me.

Then the psalmist makes the appeal more personal as he starts to describe his enemies so that God knows how bad they are and how much the psalmist is in danger:

> I say to the Lord, "You are my God;
>> give ear, O Lord, to the voice of my supplications."
> O Lord, my Lord, my strong deliverer,
>> you have covered my head in the day of battle.
> Do not grant, O Lord, the desires of the wicked;
>> do not further their evil plot.

The psalmist reminds God of his goodness and strength:

> Those who surround me lift up their heads;
>> let the mischief of their lips overwhelm them!
> Let burning coals fall on them!
>> Let them be flung into pits, no more to rise!
> Do not let the slanderer be established in the land;
>> let evil speedily hunt down the violent!

Now the psalmist asks God to punish his enemy, to destroy him with violence:

> I know that the Lord maintains the cause of the needy,
>> and executes justice for the poor.
> Surely the righteous shall give thanks to your name;
>> the upright shall live in your presence.

The psalmist expresses his faith in God's goodness and offers God a reward of thanks if God does his job and helps him.

This is the structure of most of the psalms of lament. They include a call for punishment; a curse on their enemy. Take, for example, Psalm 58:6–8:

> O God, break the teeth in their mouths;
>> tear out the fangs of the young lions, O Lord!
> Let them vanish like water that runs away;
>> like grass let them be trodden down and wither.
> Let them be like the snail that dissolves into slime;
>> like the untimely birth that never sees the sun.

One time a friend of mine, a deacon who was being sued by his former business partner of twenty years, called me. We were talking about his troubles and he said, "Isn't Psalm 58 great?" I asked him what he meant. He told me one of the ways he got through this terrible time in his life was every morning he prayed Psalm 58! We see the same pattern in verses 19–24 of Psalm 139:

> O that you would kill the wicked, O God,
>   and that the bloodthirsty would depart from me—
> those who speak of you maliciously,
>   and lift themselves up against you for evil!
> Do I not hate those who hate you, O LORD?
>   And do I not loathe those who rise up against you?
> I hate them with perfect hatred;
>   I count them my enemies.
> Search me, O God, and know my heart;
>   test me and know my thoughts.
> See if there is any wicked way in me,
>   and lead me in the way everlasting.

Because I needed one, I wrote a psalm of lament of my own:

> [prayer]Dear God, I'm sorry I was out
> when you called,
> out of my mind,
> laying a trap
> to smash the head
> of my enemy against a rock.
> I forgot that you said,
> "Vengeance is mine,"
> not mine.
> Now I'm back,
> but I need you to listen to me:
> the bully is breaking my back,
> so I need you to break him
> and restore some semblance of justice.

His friends speak against me.
I need you to break their teeth.
Here, you hold my vengeance.
I've got better things to do.
I don't really have time to hate.
Besides, it's nearly impossible
to get the bloodstains out.
Vengeance is your job;
mine is keeping my laundry clean.

In my psalm of lament I emphasize the point of praying this kind of prayer. You want to put the vengeance that you feel in your heart into God's hands. You want to let God take care of punishing your enemy, giving that job to God so that you can get on with your life.

You may want to write your own psalm of lament. Tell God your troubles, ask for God's help, let God take care of punishing your enemy, and then focus on doing good in your life.

This is a big step in forgiveness: letting go of bitterness toward the other person so that you can start to let in some sort of empathy for the other person.

Surrender

You have looked deeply at the hurt, delved into the truth of what happened and the facts and the feelings. You've tried to understand what was going on with the other person. If you couldn't have full empathy, compassion for the person, at least you have *some* sympathy; you wouldn't want to be that poor wretch. Now it's time to tell the story differently. You see things differently, so tell the story differently.

There is surrender here, a letting go of the past way of seeing what happened, a letting go of feeling like a victim. Surrender is a strategic decision that a leader makes to save his or her life and the lives of the people around him or her. Surrender is a willingness to change.

This is a good time to ask yourself: would I rather be right or happy? You can grind your jaw in righteousness and give yourself a headache, or you can release your need for restitution and relax into a freer life.

You can surrender to God. You've heard the phrase, "Let Go and Let God." Surrender the hurt feelings and resentment to God and ask God to help you. Write a psalm of lament of your own, and then pray it and mean it.

CHAPTER EIGHT

TELL THE STORY DIFFERENTLY

The stories you and others tell help shape society, spirituality, and your own story. For example, stories of the War of Independence, George Washington's character, immigrants coming to America, the frontier spirit of pioneers, the independence of cowboys, the honor and humor of Abraham Lincoln, the sacrifices of the "Greatest Generation" during World War II, and the women who have fought and continue to fight for equal rights all contribute to how Americans think of themselves.

The stories of the Hebrew Scriptures shape Jewish religion; the stories of Mohammed shape Islam; the stories told of the life of Jesus shape the Christian religion. The story of Jesus as a healer tells you to be a healer, too. The story of how Jesus met evil with goodness reminds you to do the same. The story of Jesus who forgave sins tells you about God's mercy and how you are to behave with similar mercy to those who hurt you.

The stories you tell about yourself form your identity, your personal stories shape your soul. If you want to change something, you have to tell a different story.

WHY TELL THE STORY DIFFERENTLY?

Stories that end in sadness are a tragedy. Stories that end in forgiveness are a triumph. Would you rather see your life as a tragedy or a triumph?

You may have never told the story of a hurt to anyone else. Maybe you don't need to. Maybe there is some good reason you don't want to tell your story. Still, you can tell the story to yourself as a story of triumph rather than of tragedy. There is one basic way to climb out of the rut of your story and that is to tell the story differently.

You can change the story "Jake hurt me and I'm hurt" to "Jake hurt me and I was hurt but I've forgiven him." Forgiveness can turn your story of tragedy into a story of triumph.

Lay Down the Shovel and Get Out a Ladder

When you have been hurt, sometimes you may keep the story to yourself. Some people are private and keep their own counsel. Sometimes you may feel ashamed of something and not want to discuss it with others. More often than not you want to tell your story. You want to talk through your trauma. You share the pain in the hope of finding some sympathy. You share the pain in the hope of finding some healing.

When you tell your story fueled by resentment, regret, and revenge, you don't diminish the pain; you just keep the pain fresh. You tell your pain to your friends to find support and sympathy, but you don't escape your pain. You vent your anger in the hope it will go away, but it doesn't. You just keep your revenge engine revved.

Old-school psychology encouraged *catharsis*, that is, venting anger to discard it. Venting anger can help you discover what makes you angry. Such catharsis can help you get out of a funk. Sometimes, your anger goes underground and turns into sadness. When you get in touch with the anger underneath the sadness, then you can at least get out of sad and into mad and start to move on. When you know the source of your anger, then you can disclose your anger and move to discard it. The problem comes not when you vent anger to discover it, but in continuing to vent and vent and vent. You tell the story of your hurt over and over again.

Current thinking in psychology says that venting your anger in such a way just keeps the anger alive, that is, you tell the same story over and over again, and in doing so, each time you keep the trauma fresh. You often cast yourself in the role of victim. You tell your victim story repeatedly, and you keep your feelings worked up, that is, you keep the stress response going. Rather than becoming stuck in the revolving door of negative feelings, you have to keep moving through the feelings and get on the other side. One way to move through the rehashed feelings is to tell the story differently.

TELLING THE STORY DIFFERENTLY

What you want to do is turn a story of tragedy into a story of triumph. One way to start to tell the story differently is to take a stance of goodwill toward the person who hurt you. If you assume ill toward the person, you are for certain going to make the person into a villain and yourself into a victim. When you assume goodwill toward the person, that is, try to understand the person in some positive light, then you are planting the seed of empathy.

I once talked with a woman whose mother had to be put in a nursing home. She told me that her mother had severe dementia and could not be cared for at home. The woman's father and mother had been married nearly fifty years, and after the father placed his wife in the nursing home, he brought another woman into his home to live with him. The daughter was outraged at this injustice toward her mother. Finally, in order to let go of her anger, she had to conclude that her father was acting out of grief. He wasn't trying to disrespect his wife; rather, he was trying to escape from his own sense of loss. She assumed a stance of goodwill toward her father and was better able to understand the situation from his point of view—that it was not an affront to her mother but a way for her father to deal with his grief.

Two Sides to the Story

You might ask yourself: are you a victim or a participant?

A cardinal rule of journalism or the judicial system is that every story has at least two sides. A wise judge or ethical journalist seeks to determine a balanced telling of the story to get at the truth of what happened. It's important for you to tell your story not only from your perspective but from the perspective of the one who hurt you.

Before going any further, it is important to recognize the difference between a story where you are a pure victim and where you are a participant. If you are walking along the road and are hit by a drunk driver, then you are a pure victim. You bear no responsibility for what happened other than being in the wrong place at the wrong time.

If you were sexually abused as a child by an adult, you were a victim. There is no fault in you for the adult's pathological behavior. If the charming man or woman you wed begins to beat you after you are married, you are a victim. There is no excuse for physical violence in a marriage. The other person is dangerous and it's not your fault. Continuing to live with the person under the banner of forgiveness is not what Christ is calling you to do. Christ calls you to sacrifice at the altar of goodness, not for the sake of another person's pathology.

If the hurt you feel grew out of an ongoing relationship, such as with a family member, spouse, or friend, then in some way you are a participant and you have some responsibility in the relationship. This is what is worth examining. What is the other person's part in what happened and what is your part in it?

An Exercise in Telling Both Sides of the Story

Try this exercise in telling the story differently, from both sides. It is an exercise in honesty and empathy.

Think of a situation in which you would like to forgive or be forgiven. Write about the situation from your perspective. Then write about it from the other person's perspective. Then answer the following questions:

How do the stories differ?
How do you two differ as people?
How does the other person treat you now?
How do you treat the other person now?
How would you like to be treated by the other person?
How do you think the other person would like to be
    treated?

Looking deeply at the situation from both sides helps you to understand yourself and how you relate to others. What are the unwritten rules of the family you were born into? What sort of people are you attracted to? Do you get angry and fight, or do you become quiet and acquiesce?

Looking deeply at the situation from both sides is an exercise in understanding the other person. Why does the other person react the way he does? What's her family history and what were the unwritten rules of behavior she learned? How does he behave when he is relaxed, and how does he behave when he is under stress? These are just a few of the questions to examine. The point is to try to see the situation deeply.

Sometimes it's a matter of style: you are spontaneous and the other person is a planner; you are informal and he is formal; you care about feelings and she cares about logic.

Tell the Story to Someone Supportive

It helps to tell the story to someone who can help you see your story in a different way. Tell the story to someone you consider to be a healer, that is, an insightful friend, a religious counselor, a professional therapist, someone who can help you to reframe the story and get out of the rut you are in.

Telling yourself you won't think about the hurt, that you won't dwell on revenge, simply doesn't work. In fact, it's a surefire way to stoke the fire. You can't just banish thoughts from your mind; the more you try the more the thoughts come back. The more you tell yourself or someone tells you "Don't think about chocolate donuts. Really, stop thinking about a nice, sweet, plump donut with a thick glaze of chocolate. Stop!" the more you will think about that donut.

Rather than have your inner thoughts roll around in your head, you need to bring them into the external world and disclose your thoughts so you can change them. The answer is not to stop thinking about the hurt but to think and talk about it differently.

As you go back into your story, you need to go in gently. Let your primary attitude be affectionate attention and examine the past like an archeologist, a person who carefully lifts up an object to inspect it, brushes it off, and examines it carefully to see what can be discovered about the object. Be your own kind friend as you examine what happened. If you are to learn empathy for others, you need to start with compassion toward yourself.

Some things are important and some things fall into the "life is too short to fight about" category. One way to tell the story differently is to change your focus of what you want. Ask yourself: is the thing that I am at odds about worth the anguish it's causing me? Would I rather be right or happy?

Once you get some distance between you and the hurt, when the pain is not so fresh and you can start to look back on it, you might refocus your attention from the problem to the resolution. You can ask yourself: have I learned anything?

I don't like conflict and avoid it if I can. The problem with this is that sometimes avoiding conflict is like not cleaning a cut because you don't like the sight of blood. The danger is that the cut can become infected.

A story from a workshop I led illustrates well the problem. A supervisor shared that he had the same problem of wanting to avoid conflict. He told the story of one of his employees who was abusive and offensive to other members of the team, making inappropriate remarks to young women on the staff, taking two parking places with his car, leaving trash from his meals for other people to clean up, making excuses for why he wasn't getting his work done, and yelling at people when they didn't do what he wanted.

Because the supervisor didn't want to take on this bully, the office became a sad and chaotic place; everyone that worked there felt unhappy and afraid. The team members eventually became angry with the supervisor for not confronting the offending employee. Ignoring the problem wasn't working. The supervisor wrote memos and had long meetings, but things didn't change. The supervisor tried to reason with the bully employee, to understand things from his point of view and placate him. But nothing changed and the situation got worse. The supervisor's flaw in not wanting to deal with conflict led to chaos and unhappiness for others.

Finally, the supervisor fired the employee, even though the employee threatened a lawsuit. With the bully employee gone, morale in the office improved greatly, and the other employees worked without distraction or fear of threats. The supervisor had learned a valuable and lasting lesson—don't back away from conflict because doing so just hurt himself and the people around him. Now he can look back and see that he's grown as a supervisor and as a person.

When he asked himself, "What have I learned?" the answer he reported was "Don't back down from a bully." When he asked the question, "How have I grown?" he said he is now more willing to confront bad or difficult situations sooner rather than later.

Bring God into the Story

Another question to ask is: how is God at work in the situation?

Religious people will call the transcendent, that which exists and is beyond them, God. Others will call the transcendent, "the Divine," "the oneness of soul," "higher power." However you conceptualize this power beyond yourself, remember to invite the Divine in.

How does Jesus see the story?

You have heard that it was said, "You shall love your neighbor and hate your enemy." But I say to you, Love your enemies and pray for those who persecute you, so that you may be children of your Father in heaven; for he makes his sun rise on the evil and on the good, and sends rain on the righteous and on the unrighteous. (Matt 5:43–45)

Simply put, bring God into your story. Invite God in to remind you, that is, to give you a new mind. Ask God to show you God's calm thought about the situation, rather than your boiling thoughts.

You want to invite God in as a healer. You want to invite God in to give you the power to get beyond the negative place you are in and into a new place. You can tell the story over and over again until you are in a rut that looks a lot like a grave, or you can climb out of the old story. You must lay down the shovel and get a ladder. Rather than digging deeper in the hurt, you must start to climb to a healing place. God is the one who can turn your tragic story into a redemption story. The Scripture story of Joseph and his brothers (see Genesis) illustrates how seeing God in the situation makes all the difference in the world.

In the story of Joseph and his brothers, Jacob, the grandson of Abraham, had twelve sons by two wives: ten sons were with Leah, and two sons—Joseph and Benjamin, the youngest—were with Rachel. Joseph and Benjamin were Jacob's favorites. The other ten brothers felt jealous of Joseph because he was favored by Jacob. Joseph, always described as a dreamer, experienced dreams that showed that he would become the leader of his brothers. When he told his brothers about the dreams, they resented him even more.

One day, when the brothers were in the fields with the flocks at Shechem, they saw Joseph coming at a distance. All their sibling rivalry stirred to a rage and they decided to kill Joseph. Reuben, the eldest brother, didn't share their murderous intent. He directed the other brothers to throw Joseph into a cistern. Reuben intended to come back for

Joseph, but before he could return, the other brothers sold Joseph into slavery. Joseph was taken to Egypt where his power to interpret dreams landed him a position as the prime minister to Pharaoh. When a famine came, Joseph's brothers journeyed to Egypt. When the brothers came to Joseph for grain, he hid his identity from them and by subterfuge got them to bring their youngest brother, Benjamin, to him.

Finally, Joseph revealed himself to his brothers. He said that he loved them and he forgave them, and they were reconciled. Because Joseph was the prime minister of the country, he took care of his family so they wouldn't starve and so made his father's last years happy ones. After Jacob died, Joseph's brothers became afraid that Joseph might now try and seek revenge upon them:

> "What if Joseph still bears a grudge against us and pays us back in full for all the wrong that we did to him?" *Even though you intended to do harm to me, God intended it for good, in order to preserve a numerous people* [emphasis added]....So have no fear; I myself will provide for you and your little ones." In this way he reassured them, speaking kindly to them. (Gen 50:15, 20, 21)

The story of Joseph and his brothers is one of envy, sibling rivalry, betrayal, attempted murder, being sold into slavery, the hand of God entering one's life, triumph over adversity, the possibility of revenge, salvation, and reconciliation. It is a powerful and universal story of how, with God's help, tragedy can be turned into salvation. It is the same for you—your tragedies in life can be transformed. You get to tell the story differently, and what makes the difference is the presence of God in your story.

The Crucifixion Story

The story of Jesus' crucifixion is the greatest tragedy in history. The best of men, the most innocent man, is cruelly tortured, humiliated, and executed. In Luke's Gospel, this tragedy becomes a story of forgiveness. Jesus forgives first the ones who persecuted him and then extends that forgiveness to someone who told the truth of his situation and asked for forgiveness.

In Luke 23:34, Jesus cries out to God, "Father, forgive them; for they do not know what they are doing." Jesus forgives those who are torturing him to death.

Luke continues with the story of the two criminals who were crucified with Jesus (23:39–43). One of the criminals hanging next to Jesus hurled a desperate abuse at Jesus, saying, "Are you not the Messiah? Save yourself and us!" But the other criminal answered, and rebuking him said, "Do you not fear God, since you are under the same sentence of condemnation? And we indeed have been condemned justly, for we are getting what we deserve for our deeds, but this man has done nothing wrong." He went on to say, "Jesus, remember me when you come into your kingdom." Jesus said to him, "Truly I tell you, today you will be with me in Paradise."

The good thief is a good model for looking at the truth of a situation and asking for God's help and then looking to see how God will be there for you.

Your story of tragedy can be turned into a redemption story. Tragedies can be transformed. What makes the difference is the presence of God in your story. God has already forgiven you and wants you to forgive others.

The Empty Tomb

You can find an example of telling the story differently at the end of Jesus' story in the Gospel of Matthew.

After the sabbath, as the first day of the week was dawning, Mary Magdalene and the other Mary went to see the tomb. And suddenly there was a great earthquake; for an angel of the Lord, descending from heaven, came and rolled back the stone and sat on it. His appearance was like lightning, and his clothing white as snow. For fear of him the guards shook and became like dead men. But the angel said to the women, "Do not be afraid; I know that you are looking for Jesus who was crucified. He is not here; for he has been raised, as he said. Come, see the place where he lay. Then go quickly and tell his disciples, 'He has been raised from the dead, and indeed he is going ahead of you to Galilee; there you will see him.' This is my message for you." So they left the tomb quickly with fear and great joy, and ran to tell his disciples. Suddenly Jesus met them and said, "Greetings!" And they came to him, took hold of his feet, and worshiped him. Then Jesus said to them, "Do not be afraid; go and tell my brothers to go to Galilee; there they will see me."

While they were going, some of the guard went into the city and told to the chief priests everything that had happened. After the priests had assembled with the elders, they devised a plan to give a large sum of money to the soldiers, telling them, "You must say, 'His disciples came by night and stole him away while we were asleep.' If this

comes to the governor's ears, we will satisfy him
and keep you out of trouble." So they took the
money and did as they were directed. And this
story is still told among the Jews to this day. (Matt
28:1–15)

The story of the empty tomb is told in two different ways: the
disciples told it as the resurrection story. The chief priests
told it as a story of deceit. One story is a triumph; the other
is a tragedy. Which way you chose to believe the story makes
all the difference. How you tell the story shapes your spirituality and yourself.

The disciples of Jesus Christ, then and now, believe the
story of the empty tomb as a story of hope, a story about new
life coming out of death. Believers in Jesus can chose to tell
their own stories in the light of Jesus' story. There is always
hope that a new life can emerge from tragedy; new strength
can come out of suffering. Availing ourselves of the grace of
the resurrection, we can choose to tell the story of some
transgression so that the final chapter is forgiveness.

CHAPTER NINE

GIVE FORGIVENESS FREELY

The fourth step in letting go of a grudge is **Give Forgiveness Freely**. You give forgiveness as a gift. The person who hurt you doesn't deserve your forgiveness, that's why it's a gift. You don't have to feel forgiving; you simply make a decision to forgive.

HONORING YOUR FEELINGS OF INJUSTICE

Forgiveness allows you move from negative feelings of hurt, sadness, anger, and resentment toward positive feelings of understanding, compassion, and peace. Before you decide to forgive, you may have to honor the feelings of injustice, that you have been violated. It helps when the other person apologizes and wants you to forgive him or her.

During a forgiveness workshop at a church that had its own school, someone told me about the third-grade teacher, who had a rule about forgiveness in her classroom. The rule went this way: a child who hurt another child had to ask for forgiveness, and the hurt child had to give forgiveness. But the hurt child didn't have to give it right away. Whenever one child hurt another child, the offender had to go to the offended one, ask for forgiveness, and use a forgiveness formula in which the offender stated the offense: "Please for-

give me for...." The offended child could choose to say, "I forgive you for...," stating the offense, or say, "No. I'm still mad
at you. I don't forgive you. Come back another day and ask
again." In this case, the transgressor had to come back the
next day and ask again for forgiveness and keep asking until
he or she was forgiven.

Usually, the longer the apology dragged out, the more
anxious the offender became. After a few days, the offender
was begging to be forgiven, because it was so difficult to live
in a state of unforgiveness. The teacher's rule about forgiveness taught children that their actions have consequences.
They also learned to honor their feelings. If they didn't feel
emotional forgiveness, they didn't have to pretend they did.
They didn't offer forgiveness until they felt satisfied that the
other person was truly sorry for what he or she did and had
earned forgiveness. The children in this third-grade classroom learned to honor their feelings and the value of forgiveness. Forgiveness is not something that is cheaply given.

When a child chooses not to forgive they are recognizing their violated sense of justice, they are honoring their
hurt feelings. With each passing day and each apology their
hurt feelings lessen and when they feel emotional forgiveness then they decide to offer forgiveness to the offending
child. This chapter looks at two stages of forgiveness: decisional forgiveness and emotional forgiveness.

Exercises to Describe Emotional Forgiveness

Sometimes you might find it helpful to write out your
feelings, perhaps in a poem or short essay, responding to the
question of what emotional forgiveness would feel like.
Here's an example of such a poem:

Sail Away

The sleek white sailboat is ready to fly
but for the fouled rope tethered to the hulk.
Sawing each strand of regret, one by one,
with the edge of forgiveness,
the rush of freedom
revenge recedes in the distance.

Another exercise, *The Lady Macbeth Exercise*, was taught to me by Dr. Everett Worthington. In this exercise, you will need to write in ink on your hand the name of the person who hurt you. If it is likely the offending person (your boss or spouse, for example) will see your hand, then you should use an initial or code. Each time you see the ink on your hand, you say a prayer for the person. The prayer will help you move toward emotional forgiveness. Each time you wash your hand, the name will get fainter, but you can still see it—until the ink has washed off and you no longer see the name. That's the way it is with emotional forgiveness: the negative feelings fade over time. And they *do* fade.

Deciding to Forgive

You can't control what the other person has done to you, but you can control your reaction to it. You can decide of your own free will to forgive. What forgiveness means is to renounce revenge and release the person from any emotional debt you feel they owe you. Remember the Golden Rule: you treat them as you would want to be treated.

First, you decide to forgive, and then you live with your decision. The decision is a giant step in the right direction. For some hurts, particularly small ones, your decision may move you to a better emotional place; the decision will open you up to a small miracle, and you will immediately find the freedom you want. For people dealing with big hurts, however, the decision to forgive is a giant step in the right direction, but there will still be a long walk ahead before emotional forgiveness can be reached.

Moving from Decisional Forgiveness to Emotional Forgiveness

Moving from decisional to emotional forgiveness is a crucial step in which you have to work through your negative feelings. In this phase of forgiveness, you may feel anger of many colors. You may feel grief, betrayal, disappointment, loss of trust, loss of friendship, loss of financial security. Whatever the oppressive feeling, you have to acknowledge the feeling and go through it to get to the other side.

Previous chapters have talked about the movement through negative feelings. You have to be aware of the negative feeling, name it, talk to someone about it, and then give the negative feeling over to God.

Being Aware

Your mind can hide hurtful feelings to protect you. Sometimes when the pain is so great that it can disable you, you disengage from the hurtful feeling, bury it, and move on. But the weight of that feeling still burdens you. You may think you have escaped the past, but it is still dogging you. You need to be aware of the negative feeling, know that it is still there. It can help to name the feeling as previously discussed.

Talking It to Death

After you are aware of the negative feeling and name it, then you must get rid of it. One way to eliminate an unwanted feeling is to talk it to death. You don't want to talk to just anyone about your inner life. Sharing your story is taking a risk for the sake of healing. You want to make sure the person you tell is someone you can trust with your story. This is a sacred trust, a sacred encounter. When the hurt happened, you were traumatized. You may have internalized the feeling that you deserved what was done to you. If this is the case, if you have taken on a feeling of disdain for yourself, then you have to recognize this false disregard.

The first step of Look Deeply (see Chapter 6) talked about what happened. You may want to revisit that conversation and see which feelings you talked about then and which feelings are still stuck inside you. You want to do with each negative feeling what you did in the first step. Talk about the negative feelings with a supportive person who can help you come to a new self-understanding.

Giving It to God

In the Old Testament, God's people were upfront with their negative feelings. You can see this honest prayer in the psalms, especially in the psalms of lament.

Expressing murderous thoughts is not the same thing as acting on such feelings. In fact, by giving the negative feelings to God, you are asking God to take over your feelings of revenge. You express your violent feelings to God and say, "God, I've been violated, a grave injustice has occurred. Do something about it. I'm leaving it in your hands."

Of course, God being God, God can choose to exact a harsh justice on your behalf. Or, God being God, God may have a more expansive point of view toward all creatures and will choose to act in a way that is helpful to all. The important thing is that you give the violence to God so that you do not get blood on your hands.

The problem occurs when people give their lament to God and then take it back and act on it themselves. This is doubling down on a bad bet; we sin by not trusting God and we sin by exacting violence against another. Remember, forgiveness helps you more than the other person. Forgiveness lifts a burden from your spirit. You free yourself from the chronic negative feelings, from the infection of resentment that can wear down your mental and spiritual and physical health. You give the gift of forgiveness so you can be free of grief and hatred.

Moving to Emotional Forgiveness

Once you make the decision to forgive, then you can move toward emotional forgiveness. Emotional forgiveness takes time. It takes grace, right action, and persistence. Everything good starts from God's grace. The first thing to do is to ask God for the grace to forgive, ask for the willingness to be willing to give the gift of forgiveness. You pray for the willingness until you are willing to forgive. When you have even a modicum of willingness, then you move into right action.

"Right action" means you act your way into right feeling. You take actions that are going to signal to your mind how to feel about something. For instance, you kneel as a way to send a signal to your body that it is time to pray and put you in a praying mood.

You act like you have forgiven the person. That means you don't condemn the person anymore either in your own thoughts or to another person. When a negative thought about the other person comes into your mind, you move it aside. You remember why you have empathy for the person. You pray for them. You don't take any actions of revenge.

Forgiveness takes persistence. Jesus said "seventy times seven times" you are willing to forgive. Seven times a day you may want to kill the person, and seven times a day you will put aside the thought and claim God's help. You are persistent in thinking and acting in a forgiving way. Such persistence takes patience. You know the prayer, "God, give me patience—right now!" You trustingly ask God for what you need and then act patiently, persistently. You persevere in the spirituality of forgiveness.

You may experience a small miracle and be able to emotionally forgive right away, but usually it takes awhile. This kind of persistence may not be possible relying on your own inner resources; you need to ask God for help, constantly. God is an ever-present source of strength.

With emotional forgiveness, you feel differently about the person. You turn away from your negative feelings and toward positive feelings. With positive feelings you take the stress off your body, drain the poison from your brain and then relax and have some peace of mind. You know you will have achieved emotional forgiveness when you no longer want revenge and you no longer feel sad because you have different, more positive, feelings about the person. You may now even feel sympathy, compassion, or even love for the person.

TWO OTHER TYPES OF FORGIVENESS

Just as there is an important distinction between decisional forgiveness and emotional forgiveness, there is also an important distinction between two other kinds of forgiveness: conditional forgiveness and unconditional forgiveness.

Conditional Forgiveness

Conditional forgiveness means that some condition must be met before the offended person can grant forgiveness. Conditional forgiveness is what you usually mean when you think of forgiveness. Usually the condition is that the offender offers an apology. For most people forgiveness implies that an apology has been made, and perhaps some attempt at restitution has been made by the perpetrator. Very often, in many family or work situations, the hurt is mutual, and so an admission by both parties of mutual wrongdoing is given and there is mutual forgiveness.

The offended person usually wants the culprit to show remorse and express regret. The offended person may want some sort of amends to be made, that is, there has to be some compensation made for the damage caused by the offender before the offended person can agree to give them forgiveness.

Conditional forgiveness is the sort of forgiveness that you saw in the Jewish understanding expressed in *T'shuva*. In order to satisfy the demands of justice, forgiveness cannot be given until certain conditions are met, such as remorse, repentance, a direct request for forgiveness, and restitution.

In order to honor your feelings of injustice, you have the right to ask for an apology. Give the chance to satisfy the emotional debt you feel the person owes you. This may lead to an apology, forgiveness, and reconciliation. It may lead to a discussion; it may lead to an argument. It may make the situation worse. In any case, you have stood up for your self-respect and honored your sense of justice.

Of course, how you ask for an apology is important. Doing it with anger will probably elicit anger. Asking for an apology is best done after you have had a chance to let the anger energy cool, maybe talked with a trusted friend, prayed about it, and asked God for direction. Based on the inspiration for what is the best thing to do, you can move forward.

You've probably heard the difference between "I" statements and "you" statements. "I" statements are personal and based on your inner state. "You" statements sound like judgments about the other person. It's better to start out stating how you feel and why you feel that way. Here are two ways to start a conversation:

> "I felt betrayed earlier today when you presented my idea as your own to the boss. It wasn't fair and I would like an apology."
> "You stole my idea in that meeting. You told the boss it was your own. You're a liar."

Which statement do you think is going to get you the apology?

Once you receive the apology, then you can ask how the other person intends to make it right, make some sort of restitution to you. When a person does apologize to you, then you should be gracious and accept the apology and not demean the other person in the interchange. The God of justice and mercy wants both you and the other person to walk away with dignity intact.

Unconditional Forgiveness

Unconditional forgiveness is letting go, that is, letting go of anger or grief, letting go of revenge thoughts and whatever emotional or material debt you feel is owed to you. In the face of the failure of justice, that is, there is no apology or restitution, then there is only letting go. Another word for letting go is detachment. You get beyond the hurt of the past by detaching from the negative emotions. You use your desire to be free from the past and your compassion for yourself and the other person to move past the injustice into a new future where you remember differently—remembering not the pain of the hurt but the knowledge that you have forgiven.

TRICKY SITUATIONS

When the other person doesn't apologize, especially when it is a tricky situation, you may want to ask for help. If there is a lawsuit pending or possible, you need to talk to a lawyer. If the other person is a bully, with a history of abuse, then you don't want to open yourself up to being reinjured. It's a good idea to ask someone who has been down the forgiveness road which is the best way to go. Talk to a trusted person about the best way to ask for an apology.

GIVING UNCONDITIONAL FORGIVENESS

If the other person has not offered an apology or any sort of sign of peace, there is no reason for you to reach out to the person and tell him that you have forgiven him when he hasn't asked for it. The person may not accept the gift of forgiveness and may even throw it back in your face.

Perhaps you can't convey the forgiveness directly because the person is dead. In that case, you may want to visit the person's grave and have an in-the-heart conversation with the deceased. You may want to write the person a letter and then burn it as an offering to the deceased. Such rituals give your emotions a place to go and help you come to some resolution.

FORGIVE AS JESUS TAUGHT

With unconditional forgiveness the person who has been injured places no preconditions on granting forgiveness. You forgive without an apology being offered. This is the sort of forgiveness Jesus showed us from the cross: "Father, forgive them; for they do not know what they are doing" (Luke 23:34).

Notice what Jesus does. He doesn't forgive the men who betrayed him, mocked him, whipped him, stuck a crown of thorns in his head, and nailed him to the cross. What Jesus says on the cross is not a statement of forgiveness directed to those hurting him. What Jesus says is a prayer that models what he taught: "Pray for those who persecute you." He asks God to forgive the persecutors.

A key practice in letting go is to pray for the person, situation, or institution that hurt you. Invite God into the situation. Ask God to forgive the person and to help you let go of your pain.

PARDON

Another part of unconditional forgiveness is to pardon. Pardoning someone is the decision to forgo any emotional or material restitution the person owes you. Acting with pardon is when you are owed a debt, but you write off the debt and don't demand that it be paid back. You act like a judge who has let a criminal go free, not because the person isn't guilty, not because the person doesn't deserve punishment, but because of mercy.

GIVE WHAT YOU HAVE BEEN GIVEN

To give the gift of forgiveness you have to do something, take action, not just think about it. "Give" is an active verb. The first thing to do is to ask for help. You ask God for the grace to forgive. Christians believe that we are able to offer ordinary and heroic forgiveness because we have been forgiven greatly. "We love because he first loved us" (1 John 4:19).

God has given you the gift of forgiveness and requires you to give it to others. It is hard to let go of your hurt. It is hard to release the gift of forgiveness from your hands and offer it to another. It's good to remember that you give forgiveness when it's not deserved—that's why it's a gift. You bless the person as God has blessed you. The power to forgive comes from God. You don't forgive, God forgives through you. Forgiveness is a miracle, and you need God's grace to work miracles.

COMMIT TO BEING
A FORGIVING PERSON

The gift of forgiveness is not a one-time gift but a way of life. To truly grow into your divinely appointed human nature, you need to commit to being a forgiving person, to becoming more like our merciful and just God.

As you experience the lightening of the burden of unforgiveness, you continue to commit to forgiveness. Commit to yourself that forgiveness is a spiritual path you choose to walk that will lead you to God. The divine spark in you will join with the flame of God.

Exercise for Becoming a More Forgiving Person

Every day, read a Scripture passage that is particularly meaningful to you. Read it to remind yourself to be a forgiving person; read it until it is planted in your heart. Here are some samples:

Father, forgive them; for they do not know what they are doing. (Luke 23:34)

Put away from you all bitterness and wrath and anger and wrangling and slander, together with all malice, and be kind to one another, tenderhearted, forgiving one another, as God in Christ has forgiven you. (Eph 4:31–32)

As God's chosen ones, holy and beloved, clothe yourselves with compassion, kindness, humility, meekness, and patience. Bear with one another and, if anyone has a complaint against another, forgive each other; just as the Lord has forgiven you, so you also must forgive. Above all, clothe yourselves with love, which binds everything together in perfect harmony. (Col 3:12–14)

Jesus said to them again, "Peace be with you. As the Father has sent me, so I send you." (John 20:21)

You have heard that it was said, "You shall love your neighbor and hate your enemy." But I say to you, Love your enemies and pray for those who persecute you, so that you may be children of your Father in heaven; for he makes his sun rise on the evil and on the good, and sends rain on the righteous and on the unrighteous. For if you love those who love you, what reward do you have? Do not even the tax collectors do the same? And if you greet only your brothers and sisters, what more are you doing than others? Do not even the Gentiles do the same? Be perfect, therefore, as your heavenly Father is perfect. (Matt 5:43–48)

COMMIT TO GOD

Commit to God that you will follow God's mandate to forgive. Make the commitment to God in a prayer. One way to do this is to pray the Forgiveness Prayer in the front of this book. You can say this prayer daily until it becomes second nature to you, until the values of the prayer become a part of your spiritual makeup.

COMMIT TO A TRUSTED PERSON

A way to make real the decision to commit is to tell a trusted person that you have made a commitment to forgive. In telling your forgiveness story to a trusted person, you can mention how you have come to value forgiveness and want to become a more forgiving person. You go public with your forgiveness. You can tell a trusted friend, your priest, minister, rabbi, imam, Twelve Step sponsor, spiritual teacher, therapist, or the person who cuts your hair. The point is to make your commitment more binding by telling someone else.

When you go public with forgiveness, you are saying you are serious about it. When you tell another person or put it in writing, you take an action. Remember the spiritual axiom that you act your way into right thinking and don't think your way into right action. You kneel in church to show reverence and kneeling helps you to feel reverent. When you hear the national anthem, you stand, take off your hat, and place your hand over your heart to show your patriotism. Doing so helps you feel patriotic. You show you are serious about forgiveness when you tell someone else.

DECLARATION OF FORGIVENESS

When conducting retreats, I suggest to retreatants that they write "A Declaration of Forgiveness." When the Founding Fathers of the United States wanted to declare the freedom of the Thirteen Colonies, they made their intention public with the Declaration of Independence. With a Declaration of Forgiveness, you can declare your freedom from hatred, resentment, binding anger, and hurt. You can create a written record of your intention to forgive and move on with your life. A Declaration of Forgiveness, originally credited to Dr. Everett Worthington, might look like the one in the box, but you should feel free to adapt it.

MY DECLARATION OF FORGIVENESS

On [month and date], 20[year], I, [your name], forgive [name of person you want to forgive] for [describe the hurt or offense]. Whenever I see [name of other person] or am reminded of the harm [name of other person] did to me, I will remember that I have already forgiven [name of other person]. Emotionally, I forgive [insert a number, such as 25 or 50 or 80 or 100] percent. I pledge to continue to let go of negative feelings like sadness or anger and embrace positive feelings like compassion.

Signed: [your name]

On the Declaration of Forgiveness, which should be a piece of paper and not a digital document, you should insert in the appropriate place the date, your name, the name of the person who hurt you, and what the person did to you. The first part of the Declaration of Forgiveness indicates your decision to forgive. The second part declares the quotient of your emotional forgiveness. After completing the Declaration, put it someplace where you will see it again, perhaps in your Bible or prayer book, so that you will see it when you turn to spiritual reflection and prayer.

You have written a declaration of forgiveness for yourself. You can also bring God into this act of freedom. Write out a similar declaration and give it to God. First, say a prayer, offering the declaration to God and asking for God's help. Then symbolically give it to God by burning the declaration or burying it in a place sacred to you. You can dispose of the declaration in any way that seems appropriate to you. This is God's receipt. It's a way of turning your declaration of forgiveness into a prayer.

When you have written out God's receipt and offered it to God, then you know that your declaration of forgiveness is real and is blessed. You can trust that God will help you to attain emotional forgiveness. You can find freedom from resentment and start to move toward an inner healing of the hurt done to you.

GOD'S RECEIPT

I, [*your name*], decided on [*month, day, year*] that I forgive [*name of other person*] for [*describe hurt or offense*]. Emotionally, I forgive [*insert a number such as 25 or 50 or 80 or 100*] percent and pledge with your help, God, to let go of the harm done to me and embrace your healing.

Signed: [*your name*]

CHAPTER TEN

ONE DAY AT A TIME

This is the step where one day at a time you let go of the hurt and hold onto the healing. Small and medium hurts will dim and may fade away or become neutral memories. You will look back on these lesser assaults and wonder why you let them have so much power over you; these hurts will change from transgressions to lessons. The greater hurts you will continue to remember differently as they change from being assaults to becoming mementoes of God's grace. You will make progress along the spiritual path of forgiveness, but you won't stop. One day at a time, you will grow in the spirituality of forgiveness.

FORGIVENESS IS ALWAYS IN THE PRESENT

Antoinette Bosco, the mother of seven children, lost two of them in tragedies. One son, Peter, committed suicide. The next year, 1993, another son, John, and his wife, Nancy, were gunned down in their bed by an eighteen-year-old boy with no apparent motive. Antoinette recounts her journey of forgiveness in *Radical Forgiveness*. One of her key ideas is "there is no past tense for forgiveness."

Forgiveness is a daily decision. When something horrific happens, such as what happened to Antoinette Bosco, you have to be able to renew your decision to forgive because you never know when the searing pain of your loss will resurface. Each day you must be willing to apply the medicine of forgiveness to the pain of hurt and loss.

You can expect to encounter less tragic situations regularly. You are always going to bump up against the needs, reactions, and feelings of other people in conflict with your own; it's inevitable. Some small things may be like lingering snow that eventually melts. Ignoring these, however, does not heal many conflicts. You need to address them. You may need to have a conversation and work toward what is best for everyone concerned—another way of saying "doing God's will."

When you have tried to resolve the conflict and are still left with a feeling of resentment, then one way left to bridge the injustice gap is to forgive. You have to be willing to forgive others to keep your relationships intact and to keep connected to your social community. Once you have made a decision to forgive, and even after you have achieved some degree of emotional forgiveness, old feelings of regret, revenge, and recrimination may pop up, so you have to be willing to forgive on a daily basis.

Forgiveness is a way of life. Your goal is to become a more spiritual person. Your ongoing conversion is to grow into the fullness of one of God's beloved. The path of that spiritual growth is the way of forgiveness. Each day you take another step on that path; you develop a discipline of running up and down the five steps. As you persevere with the discipline, your practice deepens. You come to deeper understandings about who you are and who God is for you; you recognize your own false self, your shadow side; you can continue to call it out into the open and not be controlled by your darker thoughts. You learn to live in the light, to find a serenity and deep joy that is your heritage, even in the midst of great upheaval or personal tragedies.

TAMING THE MONSTER CRIME

The big hurt, the monstrous offense, may be held at bay, but it never goes away. How do you forget the tragic death of a loved one, the loss of a child to drugs, the betrayal of someone you were bound to by a vow? The first four steps of forgiveness get you to a place where you can act as if the hurt is healed, even if you don't feel like it. You may have to act "as if" the hurt is completely healed. You are on a mission to reconstruct your life so that you have freedom from hurt, anger, resentment, and vengeance. To do that each day, you have to practice certain strategies.

Remember Who You Are

Each day you remember who you are—a child of God. My Uncle Nick Prencipe, when his children were leaving the house, would say to them, "Remember, you are a Prencipe." He wanted his children to remember to conduct their lives in a way that honored their family name. They were related to the Prince; they lived by certain principles. You too have to remember who you are—a child of God dedicated to the spiritual discipline of forgiveness.

As a child of God you deserve to live with dignity and self-respect. You forgive yourself for being human: fallible, imperfect, and sometimes inconsistent. You recognize that you are God's child, worthy of respect but no better or worse than any of God's other kids. You are right-sized in the world, neither too big for your britches nor a shrinking violet. You deserve to be treated with respect, and you owe respect to others.

Banish the Other Demon

Previously you banished the demon you made of the other person. Now it is time to banish another pestering demon: your desire for revenge. Your thoughts of wanting to harm the other person may return. You may want to do all sorts of dastardly things to the person, from humiliating the person in public to hanging him or her in a basement. Since you may not be able to completely do away with occasional thoughts of revenge, you have to be ready to renounce those pesky desires to humiliate, hurt, maim, or kill the other person whenever they spring up. When such thoughts surface, you need to get in the habit of turning them into a blessing for the other person.

Treat the Other Person Like a Person

Treat the person who hurt you with the same respect you did prior to the offense. This is the true sign of healing. It is not an internal feeling, it is not a private intention, it is an external action. Your relationships are based on your actions, not your intentions. You make progress in healing by praying for the other person's well-being, which is a good intention on your part and a supplication to God to both help the other person and change your heart. That prayer is between you and God. The way the other person will know that you are a true human being, a natural child of God, is by your behavior, that is, how you treat him or her. "As the Father has sent me, so I send you" (John 20:21).

Here's my reflection on how the work of forgiveness is woven into the great and eternal work of God.

String Theory

"As the Father has sent me, so I send you."
Light from Light to light, you are sent
into a constant calling forth from fear
until in the Lord's service you are rent;
until "peace be with you" is your atmosphere.
Then comes the gold spiral that sends you
spun into union, the sacred matrix;
gathered into a gently pulsing web
guided by the great, light-footed weaver
you spend eternity vibrating threads
to mend lives torn and beleaguered,
with multiple strands of forgiveness.

Stay Out of Bad Neighborhoods

In your head there may be bad neighborhoods, places you shouldn't go into, especially by yourself. Vengeance is one of those neighborhoods already discussed in this book. You also don't want to keep rehashing the old transgression by talking to other people about it. This is where the forgetting part of "forgive and forget" comes in: once you have gotten to a place of healing, don't go back into the old neighborhood.

Give Yourself Hope

The obvious theological virtue behind forgiveness is charity: you are giving someone a gift; you are doing a loving action. The theological virtue that springs from forgiveness is hope. You are giving someone else a chance to start again, to make a new beginning with you. You are giving yourself the hope of having a revitalized relationship with someone. You have the hope of moving on with your life.

The success of forgiveness for you and me is hope. We want to be able to look into the future with a smile. The generation of World War II saw the Japanese as the enemy; now we see them as trading partners. Even huge hurts can be healed. Christians believe in the Paschal Mystery, that is, out of death comes resurrection; the cross of Good Friday leads to the empty tomb of Easter. You have to renew your hope daily.

If your self-esteem has been hurt by repeated transgressions against you, then you can do positive things. Perhaps you've heard, "If you want to build self-esteem, do estimable things." Being quick to forgive in daily situations is an estimable way to act. Remember, your daily exercise is to run up and down the five steps of forgiveness. Instead of being impatient with the slow person ahead of you in the checkout line, see if you can figure out what's going on inside that person. Rather than try and push past the person in line, try stepping into her shoes. Maybe she is having a bad day, or is in the first stage of dementia, or is worried about a meth-addicted adult child, or is having trouble paying bills. Maybe the person *is* an idiot; you should forgive her for being an idiot.

Envision a New Life

Hurts you suffered, the pains you endured, the vengeance you hoped to achieve were each a part of an old way of life. Now you want to have a new life, and to get there you need to envision a new way of life. If you want to change, you have to know what that change will look like for you. The following exercises will help you change into a new life.

Exercise to Envision a New Life

Take a piece of paper and draw a line down the middle. In the first column list your faults, the personality traits you don't like about yourself that get you into trouble. In the second column, opposite each of your faults, list the positive characteristics that are the opposite of these faults.

For example:

Impatient	Patient
Dishonest	Honest
Insensitive to others' feelings	Thoughtful and kind
Mean-spirited	Good-humored
Selfish	Generous

Now, write a description of yourself using the descriptions from column two. For example: Jane/John is a patient, thoughtful and kind person who is good-humored and generous. Put this description on a card and carry it in your wallet. Read the card prayerfully often. Ask God to help let go of your faults and replace them with the positive characteristics.

Exercise to Become a More Forgiving Person

To keep the five steps of forgiveness in front of you, write on a card L-E-T G-O and keep the card in your wallet. Or post a sticky note with L-E-T G-O on your bathroom mirror, refrigerator, computer, or vehicle dashboard—anywhere you will be reminded often of how to forgive.

Exercise to Envision a Positive Future

Imagine how better off you would be because you have moved past your past. How would the people around you be affected? Would they be more open to have you in their lives?

Imagine that you are free of persistent thoughts of revenge and bitterness; imagine that you feel loved; imagine that you are free to be more loving to others. What would that feel like? Ask yourself, "What's holding me back, what would it take to make me feel whole, to feel happy?" Write out what your life looks like because you have LET GO of the old and invited in the new. Now live into the new life you've envisioned for yourself.

CHAPTER ELEVEN

THE ART OF RECONCILIATION

Reconciliation is natural, even animals can make up after they've had a fight. Reconciliation is also a skill that you learn in order to do it well. You can learn principles, then artfully apply them in each situation to reweave the fabric of a torn relationship. Christians understand that reconciliation is also supernatural. You are able to change your heart and reconcile because God has reconciled with you through Jesus Christ. So reconciliation is an art, and it starts with a conversion of the heart.

Paul's Letter to the Romans says it well:

> For while we were still weak, at the right time Christ died for the ungodly. Indeed, rarely will anyone die for a righteous person—though perhaps for a good person someone might actually dare to die. But God proves his love for us in that while we still were sinners Christ died for us. (Rom 5:6–8)

You have been reconciled with God through the sacrificial love of Jesus Christ. Through the ongoing action of the Holy Spirit, you continue to be reconciled. Jesus Christ brought you back into God's good graces and you can use that union with God to extend reconciliation and peace to others. You do the work of God when you bring to union what has been divided. You are being a peacemaker when you do the work of reconciliation.

TWO KINDS OF RECONCILIATION

There are two kinds of reconciliation: vertical and horizontal. Think of the beams of Christ's cross. The upright beam connects you to God. The crossbeam connects us to other people.

We needed to be reconciled to God because we were alienated from God by sin. In justice there needed to be an atonement for sin, there needed to be some avenue of reconciliation opened between human beings and God. Jesus provided that avenue of atonement.

We are part of a history of alienation stretching back to the beginning of humanity, and we make personal choices that are at odds with the goodness of God. We need to have our relationship with God restored after it has been distorted by sin. That restoration happens through Jesus Christ.

Horizontal reconciliation is the reconciliation between human beings, between two friends who have a fight, between two imperfect family members who feud, between the victim and the offender. Because we have first been reconciled to God, the power of God is available to us to name the injustice that has been done, to name any offense we have done, to move beyond our hurt feelings and offer the gift of forgiveness. If the wrongdoer recognizes his or her transgression and apologizes, then we can move toward reconciliation.

There are many times when the line between the offended person and offender gets blurred. Very often we may wind up hitting back. In the back and forth of hurt and retribution, sometimes it's hard to tell who the victim is.

When both parties recognize mutual responsibility, then reconciliation can happen.

Reconciliation is necessary because conflict is inevitable. You want different things and have different values from others, so egos clash and the armor of each other's defenses clank.

Human beings are not meant to live in solitary confinement. We live in community. We must cooperate with others and sometimes it's just hard to figure out how to cooperate—conflict may not be either person's fault. We may not know how to cooperate in certain situations; we may think we are doing the right thing, but we don't really know.

Then there are times when pride and envy and those other nasty habits humans have rub each other the wrong way. People want different things and people fight for what they want. We aren't willing to meet halfway or, our idea of halfway is not the other person's idea of halfway. We may have different interests that are in direct conflict.

Reconciliation is the way to get beyond the conflict of interests. We may decide to agree to disagree with the other person but still want to be in relationship with the person. We see more benefits in being in relationship than in not being in relationship. We can restore a relationship after an offense as long as we are willing to try to behave in such a way as not to re-offend. We cooperate with the other person as we did before the offense.

RECONCILIATION IS A TWO-WAY STREET

Reconciliation is a two-way street. People have to travel some distance to meet each other.

Forgiveness is a one-way street. You forgive to let go of HARM: the Hurt, Anger, Resentment, and Malice that poisons your spirit. You do it for yourself, for your peace of mind and general well-being. You can do forgiveness all on your own.

Reconciliation seeks to restore the torn fabric of a relationship, to end a conflict and restore peaceful coexistence. In order for reconciliation to happen, there has to be some sort of remorse and repentance, that is, a recognition of the harm that was done, a request for forgiveness, and a pledge not to act in an offensive way again.

In reconciliation, both parties have to want to reconcile. An apology has to be offered and accepted, and there is a mutual agreement to live in peace with one another.

The basic principle with apologies is Keep It Simple. Don't offer excuses. Just say, "I'm sorry," and then say what you did and how it affected the other person. Let the offended party know you understand the consequences of your actions for his or her life. For example, "I'm sorry when I made that joke at your expense at the office party. I know it hurt your feelings." Remember that people say "I'm sorry" in different ways. Some people say it using the nice formula above; others do it by making some sort of peace offering, that is, a gift or kind action. Some say "I'm sorry" in an offhanded or oblique way; others offer a squeeze on the shoulder and say, "We're okay, right." The important thing is that they know they did something wrong and acknowledge it so you can start to rebuild trust and move on.

NOTHING IS UNFORGIVABLE, BUT SOME THINGS ARE IRRECONCILABLE

Nothing is unforgivable if you choose to forgive. You are in control of your attitude about the offense. Forgiveness means you are no longer in bondage to the event. You can choose to free yourself by giving the gift of forgiveness to yourself.

Some things, however, are irreconcilable. When someone has hurt you, you have to ask yourself if you want to open yourself up to be hurt again. You should not reconcile with abuse, violence, or injustice. You can't reconcile if the bullets are still flying. If there is no apology and the bad behavior is ongoing, there can be no reconciliation.

The reason to reconcile is so that you can live at peace with yourself and others. You reconcile to live up to a noble vision for yourself; you want to take the high road above the rugged terrain of hate. A moral reason to reconcile is because you are adding more glue to your social network. In broader religious terms, you are building up the Body of Christ. You are making visible the ministry of Christ on earth.

Forgiveness that leads to reconciliation is like what Christ did: his atonement. He brought the world at-one-ment with God, that is, created an interconnection between humans and God. Christ created the possibility for you to live in the harmony that God intends.

Reconciliation implies that there has been a change of heart and a change of behavior. If there is no change of heart, if there is still bad blood between you and the offender, if the relationship is in some way still poisonous to either person, then reconciliation should not be attempted.

Reconciliation can't happen as long as violence is going on because reconciliation is about restoring trust. Reconciliation requires an agreement to try and rebuild mutual trust. If that understanding is not shared, then any attempt at reconciliation will be frustrated.

If reconciliation just means opening yourself up to more abuse, then don't do it. Don't let someone use the language of reconciliation to cover up an ongoing injustice. That's not reconciliation; that's denial.

If there's not going to be a change and you are just going to be involved in the same behaviors, then you are just going to do more damage.

Sometimes reconciliation isn't appropriate because there is bad chemistry between two people. Some people bring out the best in you, and some people bring out the worst in you. This does not mean there has to be a judgment about who is right and who is wrong. It doesn't mean that either one of you is bad, but, rather, one or both individuals are unconscious about something in their personality and how they relate. The necessary work to look at why the relationship doesn't work hasn't been done. This may never change. Detachment, then, is the best option. There is detachment when you can be with the person and not get hooked when they drop the bait, and there is detachment when you just take yourself out of the water.

RECONCILIATION IN RITUAL

Rituals can be powerful ways to achieve reconciliation, both practically and emotionally. Rituals are a way to achieve reconciliation in a symbolic way when it can't be achieved in a personal, direct way, such as when a person you want to reconcile with has died. For example, you could go to the deceased's grave and read a letter that expresses your forgiveness for the way the person hurt you.

When you have done harm in a general way and there is no specific person to apologize to, when you have a sense that you have sinned but are not sure who was hurt by it directly, then you can contain your apology in the safe container of the sacrament of reconciliation. This is the ritual many Catholics and other Christians use to ask God to forgive you for the sins you have committed against God's dignity and against God's creatures.

Truth and reconciliation commissions are ways to invite people who have hurt fellow citizens to reconcile with those they have damaged. It is more than a symbol. Victims get to have their story heard, often with the perpetrators in the room. This in itself can be healing. The victims are heard by authorities and their peers; they can expose the injustice and unburden themselves of their private trauma by making it public. Their truth is heard. If the perpetrator is present, then he or she is confronted with the injustice, and, in some models, can avoid prosecution by the courts if he or she tells the truth and apologizes. Perpetrators have to admit to what they did wrong and face the victims of their cruelty. They have to face the consequences of their actions. This model achieves much of what is envisioned by *T'shuva*.

Reconciliation Ritual

In the novel *The Secret Life of Bees* by Sue Monk Kidd (and film by Gina Prince Bythwood), we meet the three Boatwright sisters: May, June, and August. May Boatwright, whose feelings are so sensitive that she often bursts into tears when she sees or remembers something sad, uses a ritual when her feelings overwhelm her. She goes to a stone wall on their farm and writes on a scrap of paper whatever is troubling her. She then leaves the paper as a prayer tucked into the wall. This ritual helps her to resolve the expression of her feelings.

August explains to the lead character, Lili Owens, that the sisters created this ritual for May from observing how pilgrims use the Western Wall in Jerusalem. August tells Lili that Jews come from all over the world to pray at this wall, the only remaining structure of the Temple of Jerusalem that was destroyed by the Roman army in AD 70.

Writing out a prayer and leaving it for God can be a way for you to express forgiveness toward God, yourself, and others. It allows you to act out in a concrete way what you are feeling. When you turn an internal feeling into an external action, you are better able to move beyond the feeling. Then you can turn your attention to a different perception of your world. As the Letter to the Philippians says:

> Finally, beloved, whatever is true, whatever is honorable, whatever is just, whatever is pure, whatever is pleasing, whatever is commendable, if there is any excellence and if there is anything worthy of praise, think about these things. Keep on doing the things that you have learned and received and heard and seen in me, and the God of peace will be with you. (Phil 4:8–9)

Focus on what is worthwhile and act according to these worthwhile intentions and let God work through you for a greater good.

RECONCILIATION IS COMPASSION IN ACTION

As talked about previously, one practical way to achieve forgiveness and move toward reconciliation is to pray for the person who hurt you. Hold the thought of the person while you ask God to bless him or her. You then act according to this prayer, and when you talk about the person, you don't condemn him or her. In your actions you don't avoid the other person, unless of course the person is dangerous in some way. You treat the person as you did prior to when the offense against you occurred. You renew the relationship. You can renew the relationship because you have been made new by Christ.

The Second Letter to the Corinthians relates that God reconciled the world to himself in Christ:

> So if anyone is in Christ, there is a new creation: everything old has passed away; see, everything has become new! All this is from God, who reconciled us to himself through Christ, and has given us the ministry of reconciliation; that is, in Christ God was reconciling the world to himself, not counting their trespasses against them, and entrusting the message of reconciliation to us. So we are ambassadors for Christ, since God is making his appeal through us. (2 Cor 5:17–20a)

You are one of God's ambassadors of reconciliation sent to build peace in the world. Reconciliation is an art, and, like an artist creating a sacred image, you start with prayer. You invite the Holy Spirit to lead you as you do the work of God and create peace by doing the work of reconciliation.

CONCLUSION

Jesus Christ came to reconcile humanity to God and one another. It is up to us to each decide to participate in this work of Christ. We participate in this saving work when we forgive. We help complete this saving work when we reconcile. We claim and use God's mercy when we forgive. We claim God's power when we use the grace given to us in Jesus Christ to reconcile. We do this for the good of others and for our own good.

God wants us to live in the dignity that is the birthright of a child of God. God wants us to live with joy, the joy that is ours because of our loving relationship with God. God wants us to be free. Why live in the prison of unforgiveness when the way out is before you? You have the key to let yourself out, you have the power from God to take the steps necessary to forgive and free yourself. When it's the right time and if it's the right thing, you can also work toward reconciliation. In reconciliation, we will know a double embrace; we will experience the restoration of a relationship and the love of God.